OKLAHOMA'S
HAUNTED
ROUTE 66

TANYA McCOY

Haunted
America

Published by Haunted America
A division of The History Press
Charleston, SC
www.historypress.com

Back cover: Museum of Pioneer History, Chandler, Oklahoma.

Unless otherwise noted, all images are courtesy of the author.

First published 2023

Manufactured in the United States

ISBN 9781467154147

Library of Congress Control Number: 2023937195

In loving memory of John L. McCoy (1948–2012)

CONTENTS

CONTENTS

ACKNOWLEDGEMENTS

I dedicated one of my first books to my father, but it only seemed appropriate that I should also dedicate this one to him. His love of travel, along both the highways and railways, kept him actively on my mind throughout the development of this book. Due to his PTSD from his time serving in the Vietnam War, we moved frequently in my younger years. Our family theme song was "On the Road Again" by Willie Nelson. It appears I have inherited his love of travel as well as his love of history—not only the history of my Cherokee lineage but also the history and development of American railways. (Unlike my father, I have no desire to jump in a railcar and hobo hours away, then call my spouse to come pick me up!) I feel comfort as I travel along historic highways, because I know I still carry a piece of him with me. I miss you more every day. Until we meet again, daddy—I love you. Your baby girl, "Pug."

I also want to thank all of those who helped me during the research process of this book: My traveling partner and research assistant as well as my loving husband, Clinton Womack. My other travel buddies and researchers, Nguyet Williams, Amy McCue and Stacey Price. My paranormal team members, who are always amazing assets and dedicated researchers. All of the amazing residents of Oklahoma willing to share their stories for the book, and Sapulpa, Bristow, Chandler and Elk City Museums staff, who played a vital role in helping me obtain historical documents and stories for the book. I also want to thank all the haunted sites that allowed us in to conduct the research needed to give validation to some of the reports of paranormal activities. I also want to give a special shout-out to Josh Williams, for helping me proofread and edit stories as I went along. You all played a vital role in helping me complete this book, and I thank you from the bottom of my heart.

PART I

BLOODSHED AT THE BORDER

Construction of Historic Route 66 began in downtown Chicago in 1926. The route stretches 2,448 miles, ending at the pier in Santa Monica, California. It stretches across eight states, with New Mexico claiming the longest stretch of the route (487 miles); Oklahoma comes in at a close second (432 miles). The state with the fewest miles along the route is Kansas, which proudly displays its total of 11 miles among the historic records of the Route 66. Despite Kansas claiming just 11 miles of the route, they could very well be some of the bloodiest miles of road on Route 66. Before crossing the Oklahoma state line, a driver passes through the far corner of Kansas, but most people aren't aware of the history and the bloodshed that marks this smallest stretch of the route. The highway was one of the main thoroughfares during the 1930s Dust Bowl era, when many families drove west to California in search of a better living. It later became a popular vacation route and scenic drive. It still is today. Also known as the "Mother Road," this popular highway inspired the legendary song "(Get Your Kicks on) Route 66," first produced by Capitol records in 1946 and performed by several artists, including Nat "King" Cole and Chuck Berry. This stretch of highway also inspired a hit TV show, *Route 66*, about two American drifters traveling on the famous route. The show first aired in 1960 and lasted for four years, receiving a few Emmy nominations. One nomination went to a guest star on the show, Ethel Waters. It was the first Emmy nomination for an African American actress.

The story starts long before the planning of 66, when two small mining towns near Galena, Kansas, began a dispute about mining rights in the area. This dispute continued for several years, but the worst situation was yet to come. In the late 1800s and into the early 1900s, Oklahoma was considered the most dangerous state for the mining industry. Prior to statehood, mining in the Indian Territory lacked any laws, and enforcement of safety measures simply did not exist. Small mining towns began to spring up overnight throughout the eastern part of the region, funded and controlled by the railroad and mining companies, some of which were both and the same. With no committee to answer to, directors had the freedom to run their companies as they saw fit, which usually meant as profitable and as quickly as possible, no matter the risk to worker safety and health. This caused a great deal of unrest among the workers.

In 1935, a major labor dispute was initiated between the mining companies and miners belonging to the Mine, Mill and Smelter Workers union, ending with the miners going on strike. The result was hundreds of union miners becoming unemployed. In response to the strike, the mining companies simply replaced them with non-union workers organized into a company union commonly called the Blue Card Union. This resulted in a large group of the unemployed miners attempting a roadblock along Route 66. They threw rocks and sprayed bullets at passing cars. The local police force had to detour traffic from the union strike area. Alf Landon, the governor of Kansas, declared martial law in Galena. The National Guard was dispatched to calm the violent conditions. The feud and unrest continued over the next few years until violence exploded once again. On April 10, 1937, the unemployed miners, with the assistance of the Committee for Industrial Organization (CIO), were distributing leaflets for the smelter in Joplin, Missouri, when a group belonging to the Blue Card Union seized the leaflets and severely beat the unemployed workers. The next day, April 11, about five thousand Blue Card Union members met at Pitcher, Oklahoma, armed with clubs and pick handles to intercept the CIO organizers and demolish their union hall on their way to Treece and Galena to do the same. Members of the Unemployed Union had been forewarned of the approaching threat and barricaded their meeting hall. When the Blue Card Union members arrived, gunfire erupted. Nine men suffered gunshot wounds; one was fatally injured. The hall was wrecked, and all of the union records were stolen. A short time later, ten members of the CIO were arrested, along with twenty-five members of the Blue Card Union. The mining community would never be the same. In the 1970s, the mines began to dry up. The populations of many small mining towns declined. Some towns died out completely, to live on only between the pages of history books.

PART II

THE BEGINNING ROOTS OF ROUTE 66

The First World War had just ended, and the nation was entering an era of growth and expansion. With the mass production of automobiles and the desire of so many people to escape the heartache of loved ones lost to war, families began to migrate west to newer states, including former Indian Territory, now the state of Oklahoma. During the war, it became clear that there was a need for a more efficient highway system, not only for the benefit of individual travelers but also for the advancement of military infrastructure. The Good Roads Movement began in the late 1800s. Locally, a man by the name of Cyrus Avery soon became a major advocate for the development and arrival of Historic Route 66 to Oklahoma.

Avery arrived in Oklahoma as a young boy traveling with his family in a covered wagon, having left their home in Pennsylvania to start a new life in Indian Territory. Once there, he continued to make a living farming before branching out into the oil industry and engaging in various civic duties. One such duty was serving as the chairman of the state's highway commission. It was during this time that he earned the nickname that would be forever attached to his legacy: "Father of Route 66." Avery was instrumental in the formation of Route 66 through Oklahoma, ensuring that the highway found its way through his adopted home state. He was involved in the founding of the U.S. Highway Route 66 Association, which helped boost tourism along the route and played a major role in ensuring that the entire highway be paved, from Chicago to California. One

Left: Route 66 Planning Party. *Lincoln County Historical Museum, Stroud, Oklahoma.*

Below: Children working on Route 66 prior to the enacting of child-labor laws. *Dobson Museum, Miami, Oklahoma.*

campaign to raise awareness of the newest route took place in 1928, the Trans-American Footrace, also known as the "Bunion Derby." This was a race spanning more than 2,400 miles, the length of the new Route 66. It then continued on to New York to complete the journey. The event was organized by sports agent C.C. "Cash and Carry" Pyle. It was a grueling, eighty-four-day race across the country. Participants were exposed to all types of weather and conditions on the ground. A prize of $25,000 (almost $500,000 in today's economy) was offered to the winner. The race began with 199 men, but only 55 crossed

Cyrus Avery, the "Father of Route 66."

the finish line. It was one of Oklahoma's own who claimed the prize. Andy Payne, a twenty-year-old man of Cherokee heritage, received the money and title, earning him a place in history. The campaign proved to be a success, and by the end of the 1930s Route 66 had been completely paved from start to finish. It soon became known as the "Main Street of America."

1

SOME DIDN'T GET THEIR KICKS ON ROUTE 66

The development of Route 66 was supposed to help facilitate change and growth across the United States, but for some, this famous route would only continue prejudice and injustice across an already fractured nation. The Civil War ended about fifty years before the construction of this famous highway, but many travelers of African American descent found themselves facing another home-front enemy: segregation. African Americans often found themselves banned from motels, restaurants and other businesses along the route. Despite America being known as the land of the free, the freedom to travel, lodge and even buy food or gas had become difficult. The biggest obstacle they faced came to be known as "sundown towns." These were towns and cities along the route that did not welcome any "nonwhite folk" after the sun went down. Unlucky souls who found themselves in a sundown town after dark were often beaten or even murdered. Some towns had their own chapters of the Ku Klux Klan, which met regularly to ensure that their way of life and beliefs were maintained. Serving in the military and fighting alongside other soldiers during World War I didn't exempt African Americans from becoming victims of the Klan's vengeance. Jealousy, hatred and fear ignited actions that would soon lead to mob lynchings, thievery and the disgrace that was the Tulsa Massacre. It was during this time of segregation, in 1936, that a man by the name of Victor H. Green, a Black postal worker from New York City, created and published a travel guide, *The Negro Motorist Green Book*, which listed those places that

Oklahoma Ku Klux Klan. *Sapulpa Historical Museum.*

were safe for African Americans to stay, eat and shop at along the way. It remained in publication until 1966. Despite Oklahoma being a young state at the time, it had several sundown towns. It's a part of history many towns wish to forget, but we can't erase history. We can only strive to never repeat its wrongs.

PART III

MURDER AND CRIME ON OKLAHOMA'S ROUTE 66

Since this famous route first welcomed travelers in 1926, it has offered guests a lifetime of memories and adventure. But some unlucky travelers reached the end of their life's journey on Route 66. One family met such a fate in early January 1951, when an act of generosity sealed their fate. This trail of terror started along a different roadway, but the family's living nightmare soon led them to their destination on Route 66.

The Mosser family started out on a getaway to visit the father's twin brother in Albuquerque in December 1950. They left their home in Hammond, Illinois, and headed out on the famous highway toward New Mexico. On December 30, 1950, Carl Mosser mailed a postcard to his brother from Claremore, Oklahoma, where the family had stopped to eat breakfast. It would be the last time his brother ever heard from Carl. Around 11:00 a.m. that day, just outside of Luther, Oklahoma, the Mosser family came face-to-face with the devil himself: William Cook.

Known by the nickname "Billy the Cockeyed Cook," William Cook had left California just a few days before, heading back to his hometown of Joplin, Missouri, leaving a reign of terror across several states in his wake. Little did the Mosser family know that their days were numbered. William Cook had spent most of his life in foster homes after the death of his mother when he was five. His father abandoned him and his seven siblings in an old mine, leaving the children to fend for themselves. He became a ward of the state just before his tenth birthday. Billy was born with a deformed eye, making him the frequent recipient of teasing and a mark for bullies. He became resentful and was known for his nasty temper. He was only fourteen years old the first time he was arrested, for assaulting and robbing a cab driver. William spent the rest of his life in and out of jail and prison until his execution in 1952.

On that fated early morning in December, Carl Mosser offered Billy a ride, unaware of who he had just let into their lives. It would prove to be a fatal mistake for the family. Once inside, Billy pulled out a snub-nosed .37-caliber revolver and pointed it at Carl's head. He then ordered Carl to turn south, taking the family on a southern route to Texas and Wichita Falls. It was there that Carl approached a local gas station attendant, begging him to intervene and informing him that the man with the family had a gun and was going to kill them. The attendant grabbed a shotgun from behind the counter and ordered both Carl and Billy to leave. Another customer, believing Carl's plea, jumped into his truck and followed them across the Red River, following the car for almost an hour and a half, only to lose it after being shot at several times. Over the next three days, the family was forced to travel across several states, living in constant fear. Just after dark on New Year's Day 1951, the family and their assailant pulled into the south side of Joplin, passing a patrol car along the way. Carl's wife, Thelma, started to scream frantically in an attempt to gain the officer's attention. Carl screeched the car to a halt, and the three children became hysterical. The policeman was unaware of the family's plight, failing to acknowledge the scene only a few yards away, and continued on his way. The sound of gunshots filled the air as the cold and calculating killer took close aim, firing his bullets into the innocent bodies of the family members he had traveled with for three days. Even the family's beloved pet was unable to escape the evil of the man sitting with them. An innocent family of five died that day: Carl Mosser (thirty-three), Thelma (twenty-nine), Ronald (seven), Gary (five) and the youngest victim, Pamela Sue (two). Their lifeless bodies were dumped in an abandoned mine shaft in Joplin.

Once again, Cook took to the road, heading back into Oklahoma. The family's car, now riddled with bullets and stained with blood, was found abandoned on January 3 along a rural road northwest of Tulsa. Soon the events of the family's final days started to be pieced together, revealing a four-thousand-mile nightmare that lasted for three days. The investigation conducted in Tulsa was joined by over two thousand law enforcement officers and soon led to the capture of the infamous murderer as he attempted to escape through the Mexican border. He was arrested by Mexican authorities and returned to the United States to meet his fate. In a cocky tone, he asked, "Just how high do they hang them in Oklahoma?" A plea deal saved him from the death penalty in Oklahoma, and he was sentenced to three hundred years in prison for his crimes. He wouldn't be so lucky in California. He was sent there to face charges for the murder of a man from Seattle whose car he stole and for the kidnapping of an officer. Tried and convicted in California, Cook was sentenced to death. He served his final days in San Quentin. He was put to death in the gas chamber on December 12, 1952.

William Cook wasn't the only famous serial killer known to travel Route 66. The famous and deadly duo Bonnie Parker and Clyde Barrow were often seen driving the route between Oklahoma and Joplin and were known to have several hideouts along the route. They left a trail of blood along the way. A notorious cop killer, Clyde had boasted that he was going to "get" another officer in the vicinity, but it wouldn't be Clyde who claimed the duo's next victim. In fact, the criminals had become a trio, and Henry Methvin would claim the next life. That victim was Constable Cal Campbell of Commerce, Oklahoma, on April 6, 1934. Bonnie and Clyde were traveling with Methvin through Commerce when their car got stuck in the mud. Constable Campbell, along with Commerce Police Chief Percy Boyd, walked toward the car to inquire what was happening. Gunfire erupted. Campbell was killed, and Boyd was injured. The trio then kidnapped the police chief and took him into Kansas. Chief Boyd was later released at Fort Scott, Kansas, but Bonnie and Clyde's fate was already sealed. On May 23, the murderous pair's reign came to an end in Louisiana, when they met up with a large posse led by the famous Texas Ranger Frank Hamer. A flurry of bullets littered the hull of the stolen car, and Bonnie and Clyde took their last breaths. Their legend lives on, as do the stories of their criminal activities along Oklahoma's Route 66.

Many crimes have taken place along or near the famous route since its beginning. Many are well known and well documented, but a few remain unsolved to this day. One such crime was the murder of a local lawman in Depew, Oklahoma. On October 6, 1931, at approximately 5:00 a.m., the Chief of Police, George Luckett, was making his nightly rounds. As he walked through an alleyway, he was shot three times by a perpetrator wielding a shotgun. One shot hit Luckett's chest, another his neck and the third his head. Evidence at the scene led investigators to believe he either put up a fight or was dragged to the location where his body was found. His gun and gun belt were missing. Several threats had been made against his life prior to the incident, and many suspects were interviewed. But no one was convicted of the crime. He had served two years as the chief of police in Depew and left behind a wife and three children. The crime has never been solved. Does the spirit of Officer Luckett continue to walk the streets of Depew, doing his nightly rounds and continuing to watch over the residents of his beloved town? Does his spirit cry out for justice to help bring closure for his family? Such a long time since the killing, the likelihood of the assailant or assailants still being alive to face justice is not a possibility. But perhaps one day someone will come forward with information to help solve the case, allowing his spirit to find peace once and for all.

Another notorious serial killer known to have frequented the Oklahoma route was once dubbed "Public Enemy No. 1" for his frequent run-ins with the law. Charles Floyd, better known as "Pretty Boy Floyd," grew up in Akins, Oklahoma. He was one of many children belonging to a poor farmer during the Depression. Floyd had his first contact with the criminal underworld in another small town on Route 66, Vinita, Oklahoma. He started his life of crime early and landed in jail at the age of eighteen for robbery, a crime he would continue to perform until his death in July 1934. Like Bonnie and Clyde, Floyd was known by law enforcement as a bank robber and cop killer, earning him the top spot on the list of the Bureau of Investigation, later known as the Federal Bureau of Investigation (FBI). Despite his life of crime, Floyd was often seen as a modern-day Robin Hood for burning mortgage papers at the banks he robbed and only robbing ones that were insured. It is said that at times he rode along with Bonnie and Clyde and frequented many local spots along Route 66, including a speakeasy in Oklahoma City that still stands today. He was loved by the public but hated by the law. Rewards were offered for his arrest by bankers and even the governor of Oklahoma, but many residents of the state looked at him favorably, often feeding him and hiding him when needed. It was even said that in certain towns, officers would "go fishing" when they knew he was around. Floyd was nicknamed the "Gentleman Outlaw." He met his end in October 1934 in Liverpool, Ohio. His body was returned home to Akins, where he was laid to rest in the town's cemetery, leaving his ghost and his memories to forever wander Historic Route 66.

2

THE BANDIT WHO
WOULDN'T GIVE UP

Elmer McCurdy was born in 1880 to a seventeen-year-old unwed mother and a father whom Elmer never knew. Today, this isn't an unusual occurrence, but back then, a child born under such circumstances would have been considered scandalous, to say the least. So, in order to save Sadie from the embarrassment of raising an illegitimate child on her own, her brother and his wife adopted the child and allowed the young mother to stay with them. After Elmer's uncle passed away in 1890, Sadie decided to tell her son the truth. She admitted that she was his real mother and that she was unsure who his father was. Elmer did not take the news well and soon began to act out. He changed from being an unruly child to a famous western outlaw.

After the death of his mother, Elmer moved to Maine to join his grandfather and was trained in the plumbing business. It appeared that his life had finally begun to flourish. Unfortunately, his good luck was short-lived. With the passing of his grandfather and the economic depression of 1898, he once again faced a harsh life. He turned to alcohol, which made it hard for him to hold down a job. In 1907, he joined the U.S. Army for a short stint. He was trained as a machine-gun operator and worked with nitroglycerin in its use in demolition. This training helped to launch the future activities that led him to a life of crime. His life ended only a few years later when, he was fatally shot in the early morning of October 7, 1911.

What started out as a well-planned robbery ended up just the opposite. McCurdy and two other outlaws planned to stage a robbery of a Missouri-

Kansas-Texas Railroad (KATY) train that they heard would be carrying a royalty payment of $400,000 for the Osage Nation. On October 4, 1911, the group set out to intercept the train near Okesa, Oklahoma. Unfortunately for them, they boarded a passenger train by mistake. That day they got away with just $46 from the mail clerk, a few personal items, a revolver and a couple bottles of whiskey. They holed up in an old hay shed on a local ranch, licking their wounds and getting drunk on the whiskey they had stolen. While they slept and drank, a small posse of deputy sheriffs accompanied by bloodhounds tracked the trio to the hay shed. In the early morning hours, they sat in wait for the bandits to emerge. Around 7:00 a.m., shots rang out as the outlaws began shooting at the lawmen. The deputies returned fire. The report given by the deputies was that the gunfight lasted about an hour. When the smoke and dust cleared, the outlaws, including McCurdy, were found lying in the shed, their blood slowly seeping into the earth below.

With such a short-lived life of crime, you would think McCurdy's story would end there. But it's with his death that his story truly begins. McCurdy received a single gunshot wound to the chest, claiming his life. His body was taken to Pawhuska, where the local undertaker, Joseph L. Johnson, prepared his body for burial. He embalmed the body with an arsenic-based preservative, which would help keep the body preserved over a long period. When no one came forward to claim McCurdy's body or pay his bill, Johnson decided to recoup his financial loss by dressing the body in old, ragged clothes and displaying it in an old wicker casket that he displayed in his funeral home for all to see. Well, for anyone wishing to pay a nickel to see it, that is. He dubbed his exhibit "The Bandit Who Wouldn't Give Up."

The freakish exhibit became a popular sight and soon caught the attention of traveling carnival shows. Despite receiving multiple offers to purchase the body, Johnson refused to sell. It was only when two men arrived claiming to be McCurdy's long-lost brothers who wished to take his body home to California for a proper burial that Johnson parted with his sideshow moneymaker. Little did Johnson know that the two men were the Patterson brothers, owners of the Patterson Carnival Show. Instead of the body being shipped to California, the brothers shipped it to Arkansas City, Kansas, to become a sideshow attraction. McCurdy's body traveled the country with the Pattersons until 1922, when it was sold to Louis Sonney, the owner of the Traveling Crime Museum. McCurdy's body was featured along with wax replicas of famous outlaws like Bill Doolin and Jesse James.

In 1928, McCurdy's body returned to Oklahoma, joining the Trans-American Footrace, the very race that promoted and launched the opening of Route 66. His body accompanied the contestants to the finish line and spent the next fifty years off and on along the coast of California. In 1933, a film director obtained permission to use the corpse to promote his films. He set up an exhibit with McCurdy's body in movie theater lobbies across the country. With the passage of time, the corpse began to wither and shrink and soon became mummified. In 1949, Sonney passed away, and McCurdy's body and several other exhibit items were stored away in a warehouse in Los Angeles. In 1964, his body was once again loaned out to the movie industry, making an appearance in a film. In 1968, the corpse and wax figures were sold to the Hollywood Wax Museum. It was even put on display at Mount Rushmore for a short time, where it sustained wind-induced damage—the corpse lost some fingertips and the tips of the ears. It was decided that because of the damage, the corpse was too gruesome-looking to be displayed. It was returned to California, where it was used in the funhouse at the Pike Amusement Park in Long Beach.

In 1979, a TV crew was working on an episode of *The Six Million Dollar Man* when a stagehand went to move what he thought was a wax figure to a different location for filming. An arm broke off, exposing a human bone and tissue. The police were called, and the body was taken to the local coroner. The examination revealed that the cause of death was a single gunshot to the chest. In the corpse's mouth was found a 1924 penny and a ticket stub from Pike Amusement Park. Investigators followed the trail back to Dan Sonney, Louis's son. Dan was able to give the detectives the name of the corpse. Medical and dental records and a skull image created by the Los Angeles coroner's office determined that the body was that of the outlaw Elmer McCurdy. The story of McCurdy's "afterlife" soon spread across the country and was reported in various publications and TV programs. The Indian Territory Posse of Oklahoma Westerns successfully petitioned to obtain the body, and it was returned to Oklahoma for a proper burial. In 1977, the funeral procession for McCurdy made its way to the Boot Hill section of the Summit View Cemetery in Guthrie, where the outlaw was laid to rest next to the infamous Oklahoma outlaw Bill

Elmer McCurdy. *Oklahoma Historical Society.*

Doolin, the same man whose wax figure McCurdy had accompanied across the country so many years before.

McCurdy did not live long enough to witness the opening of Route 66, but he was present in the official launch of the highway along which his body would travel for decades to come. McCurdy may not have died along the route, but his body provided a chilling sight for many along their travels. Perhaps his spirit still travels freely along the route, joining so many others on the long, dark highways of Historic Route 66.

PART IV

THE TOWNS AND CITIES
ALONG OKLAHOMA ROUTE 66

3

MIAMI

Historic Coleman Theatre

Located in the heart of historic Miami, Oklahoma, along Route 66, sits a beautiful Spanish Colonial Mission building beckoning inside anyone who glances its way. When one does enter, their breath is taken away by the majestic beauty. Decorated in dark, rich hues of red in a Louis XV style, the interior beauty begins to outshine even the gloriously built exterior.

Built by George L. Coleman Sr. in 1928, the theater officially opened its doors on April 18, 1829, at a cost of $600,000 (more than $10 million today). Its hand-carved woodwork showcasing cherubs, gargoyles and dolphins can be seen throughout. Antique furniture covered in various fabrics line the walls, adding to the lure of the venue. A grand staircase extends toward the second floor, details on its railings carved into the dark, stained wood. On the second floor is a large, open walkway offering alcoves for people to sit and chat. There are also other smaller rooms. A set of smaller stairs extends into the upper seating area of the theater for those who wish to see the stage from a grander vantage point. Crystal chandeliers hang from the ceiling, adding a touch of class as they illuminate the floors below.

Unlike any other theater in the state, the Coleman Theatre could put other historic theaters around the world to shame. The care and love that it took to create the theater's details are beyond words, even for this writer. One has to see the facility in person to truly understand the feelings it evokes

Above: Historic Coleman Theatre. *Coleman Theatre, Miami, Oklahoma.*

Left: Inside Coleman Theatre. *Coleman Theatre, Miami, Oklahoma.*

in one's soul. I must admit that, if I died and decided to come back as a ghost, I would choose the Coleman Theatre to do so. So it's no wonder that the building contains a spirit it or two.

As I've mentioned in previous books, when I enter a location for the first time, I prefer to go in blind. Not physically, of course. I'm too clumsy, and with my luck I'd find myself falling from the top balcony. By blind, I mean not knowing any of the ghostly history that may or may not be attached to the location. This theater was no different. Once inside, I knew the reports of possible activity were true. You can feel the energy in the air. We were granted access to walk the floors and take pictures of the building. It simply took our breath away. As I ran my hand along the carved wooden railing of

Entryway of the Coleman Theatre, present day.

the staircase, years of history came flooding in, taking me to a time when the state was still young and its residents hopeful for a new start. This is where I met the first spirit, that of a young woman lingering in the halls in a long taffeta dress. Her bare shoulders were exposed, and a small strip of

Above: Upstairs of the Coleman Theatre, present day.

Left: Coleman Theatre, upstairs.

ruffled material was wrapped eloquently around her upper arm. Her hair was twisted and shaped in a delicate design. She stood with grace and gave off a vibe indicating that this is where she belonged.

Heading back toward the downstairs area, just outside the entryway into the theater and stage area, I found myself running into yet another ghostly presence, that of a man. Not just any man, but a large man who evidently likes to make himself known. As we completed our quick walk-through, I found my way to the concession stand to speak with some of the staff and grab a box of freshly popped popcorn. It's hard to resist popcorn when its delectable smell assaults one's nose. I was greeted by two staff members and began my inquiry into the paranormal activity in the building. At first I wasn't sure if they were open to discussing it, but when I informed them of what I saw and felt in just the small area of the building, their curiosity took hold, and we were invited into the basement area, one not often allowed to the general public, to see what we might be able to pick up there. It was a dark, damp area, so I was ecstatic to be there. We were shown down a steep set of concrete steps into the bowels of the building. We were shown the old air-conditioning system, still intact and slightly submerged in a shallow amount of water. I immediately started taking pictures. We were left alone to wander the basement. As we walked into an adjacent room, I noticed a small alcove area below the stairs. My attention was immediately drawn there, and we took more pictures. Across the way was a small half wall that connected to the outer wall of the structure. I felt as if we were being watched. The sound of a child's laughter began to fill my head. I could see a young boy running back and forth between the two locations as he ducked behind the walls, giggling, as if playing a game of hide-and-seek. Not disturbed by his presence, we went into the darker areas of the room. There I noticed an old wicker rocking chair leaning casually against the wall. Its back was missing, but its seat was intact. The chair left the impression that someone still sat there from time to time. Their energy was still felt in its fibers. In the back part of the building is a vast open room that a visitor can stand up in if they can duck down enough to enter the small doorway. Another spirit was felt in this area; unlike the others, it didn't like to make itself known, often choosing to stay tucked away in its own space below the theater.

We returned upstairs, and I began to tell the staff what I experienced and felt in the area below. My feelings were confirmed by reports that others had experienced or felt much the same thing. I felt validation that I had not simply dreamed up the things I had just experienced. Trust me when I say that, even after decades of research and investigations, I

The basement of the Coleman Theatre.

still question myself each time I think I see or feel something out of the ordinary. Knowing that others have experienced the same helps me to believe that they and I are not imagining things. Spirits continue to walk the floors of the Coleman Theatre and perhaps always will. To be honest, who can blame them? The venue offers a grand experience. Even the spirits appear welcoming, beckoning each new visitor to come through the doorway and into Oklahoma's forgotten past, a time of elegance and grace at Coleman Theatre.

An Oklahoma Hometown Hero

It's sad to see how much history can be lost and forgotten over the years. Oklahoma has seen its fair share of shaded history, mystery and mayhem, but if you dig a little deeper, you will learn about some of the amazing residents who truly make Oklahoma what it is. There is never a shortage of news about individuals harming one another or indulging in criminal activity. But with the bad there is always the good to take its place. The motto "Oklahoma Strong" represents those good people, the ones who step up to help whenever someone needs a hand. We often think about this in relation to the aftermath of tornadoes, which occur all too often in this state. But it goes beyond that. There are the silent heroes who many never see until years after the fact. One such hero is Frantie "Frances" Mae Hill of Miami, Oklahoma.

Her story comes from a chance meeting at a local dance held by the Miami Country Club in the early 1940s. America had not yet entered World War II, but it did offer its services in another way. At that time, there were only six training schools in the United States for airplane pilots. Miami was chosen to be the location for the no. 3 Spartan School of Aeronautics to train British airmen. With the war raging thousands of miles away, these schools offered a location for new cadets to learn how to fly without the threat of being shot down by enemy fire or their base being bombed. In July 1941, the school officially opened, and cadets soon began arriving. Miami citizens were quick to open their homes to these young men living far from home, offering home-cooked meals and some company to help ease their homesickness.

Frances and her husband were no different. It was at the dance that Claude, Frances's husband, met and befriended a young airman by the name of Jack Taylor. Unfortunately, like so many other brave men, Jack did not survive the war. Some young cadets the town came to know never saw combat, in some cases perishing during training. Oklahoma became their new home; their bodies were laid to rest in the Grand Army of the Republic Cemetery. During the school's four years of operation, 2,214 RAF cadets were trained there. Of these, 15 young airmen, 10 of whom were under the age of twenty-one, died during training. At the time of Jack's death, two students had already perished and were buried in the nearby cemetery. Frances noticed the poor state of their graves and decided to undertake the task of maintaining these sites in honor of their friend Jack. In her labor of love, Frances walked three miles each way from her home to tend the ever-growing number of graves of cadets who lost their lives so far from home. Not only did she tend to their graves, but she also tended to their families, often writing them and sending them pictures of the cadets' final resting places. Her work continued for the next forty years, until she could no longer manage it herself. Frances passed away in 1982 at the age of ninety. Her final wish was to be buried next to "her boys," whom she had seen to for so many years. She did so out of love and kindness, never for fame or glory. She never boasted about the medal she received in June 1947, given by His Majesty, King George IV. The award, known as the King's Medal, is given for service in the service of freedom. In fact, many residents did not know about it until after Frances's death. The love and compassion this Oklahoma woman showed made her an angel on Earth, and I have no doubt she earned her own wings and is now flying high with her boys once again.

4
VINITA

EASTERN STATE HOSPITAL FOR THE INSANE

Located approximately sixty miles northeast of Tulsa is the small town of Vinita. It became the second Cherokee town to be incorporated under the Cherokee Council. In 1898, the United States passed the Curtis Act. This law abolished all tribal courts. Vinita came under Arkansas law, which the U.S. government claimed control over, extending the territory incorporating Vinita into its jurisdiction. In 1907, the area set aside as Indian Territory, later renamed Oklahoma Territory, became the forty-sixth state. Businesses and residents soon called Vinita home. One resident later became a famous actor, Will Rogers. He would help shape the state and bring awareness to Oklahoma. As a result, many buildings and sites were named after him, including the Oklahoma City airport. He was not the only famous person to call Vinita home. Gene Autry, Olympian Jeff Bennett, rodeo cowboy Tee Woolman and TV celebrity Dr. Phil McGraw (better known as Dr. Phil) all have strong ties to this little city on the Oklahoma state line. Historic buildings line Vinita's downtown streets, transporting visitors back to Oklahoma's early years, when the state was new and life was hard. The weatherworn bricks tell the city's story of days gone by, as the wind carries the spirits of former residents across the land. The sleepy little town seems to be an uneventful place, but few people know of its dark history, found at the edge of town. It is a history some would prefer to forget, but the burning of a paper can never truly erase the history that seeps so deep into the land.

Eastern State Hospital, Vinita.

Just outside the edge of town sits a small complex, its campus cluttered with age-worn buildings sitting empty as a grave and feeling just as cold. Established by the Oklahoma legislature in 1909, the facility opened its doors to accept its first patients in 1913. Originally known as Eastern Oklahoma Hospital for the Insane, it adopted other names through the years. The final name change occurred when a part of the facility was used by the Oklahoma Correctional Center, a prison located next to the former hospital. It became known as the Northeast Oklahoma Correctional Center, where prisoners suffering from mental illness were detained to serve their time.

The land, 160 acres once owned by S.S. Cobb, then by the City of Vinita, was given to construct the facility. In 1912, the first of the buildings were completed. By 1913, patients began to arrive, initially by a special train. Three hundred patients were transferred from the Oklahoma Sanatorium in Norman to their new home in Vinita. With the depot a fair distance from the hospital, a special area was set up where wagons met patients and staff. The area was designated the Asylum Spur. The wagons were used to convey women and older gentlemen as well as any disabled people; others were made to walk to the new location.

With the ever-growing population and the need for more space, more land was acquired, and new buildings began to emerge. More dormitories were added, as well as a maximum-restraint building, staff quarters, a barn, a sewage plant, a canning plant, a fire station and a greenhouse, to name a few. The hospital became its own working town, able to produce its own food and store it for future use. By 1954, 2,600 patients were residing in the facility, along with 590 employees. By the 1960s, funding for mental health care had begun to dwindle, so the facility began to offer various outpatient services, decreasing its inpatient population. Many of the buildings closed. From 1979 to 1983, it was designated as the treatment center for all inmates of the Department of Corrections. Building number 12 was renovated to make it more secure in order to house inmates with mental disabilities in a maximum-security setting. With new laws put into place and a further decrease in funding, the facility began to close some facilities in 1999. In 2008, it shut its doors forever when the last patient was moved out. Today, the campus sits along a country road, the prison its nearby neighbor and a few small houses lining the street facing the buildings sitting in darkness. Just beyond the campus walls sits an abandoned cemetery left to the winds of time. There is no one to care for the graves of the lost souls who once called this facility home. If the rumors are true, there are many spirits who still do.

Most of us have seen a scary movie depicting the mistreatment and abuse of mentally ill patients in an asylum. From what records and reports indicate, those depictions are not far from the truth. Eastern State Hospital was no exception. Not all staff were abusive; many thought they were being helpful when doing as they were instructed or what they believed was right. Other forms of neglect and mistreatment were no fault of the staff. The blame for that falls on the state government. For over a century, the state has neglected and turned its back on the mental health of its residents. Due to a lack of funding, facilities were—and still are—not able to properly provide or train staff to care for the residents. This led to the neglect of patients. In July 1946, Mike Gorman, a journalist for the *Daily Oklahoman*, the Oklahoma City newspaper, was tasked with researching the care of patients at the facility after a reader wrote in to complain about the treatment. The mistreatment he observed began a lifetime campaign on his part. He lobbied for better treatment and care for the mentally ill. He reported on the buildings being filthy, overcrowded and understaffed. Patients were said to lie half-naked on cold stone floors, secluded in locked rooms with only a peephole to look out of. Staff were overworked and underpaid; the patient-staff ratio exceeded acceptable levels. Many patients had not stepped foot outside of their building for ten years or more due to a lack of available staff to escort them. The death rate was unacceptably high and causes of death often questionable. Improper treatment was only to be expected from staff who were overworked and offered little time and even less freedom themselves. Each staff member was expected to work thirteen-hour days with just half a day off per week. They were forced to live on the property and have meals there. They were given little pay; room and board were considered part of their compensation.

Sometimes, patients who were capable worked alongside the staff as a form of "therapy" treatment. Some family members of patients reported that their relatives were kept at the facility longer than was necessary. In one case, a family attempted to remove their mother, who had admitted herself due to major depression after the loss of a loved one. She was having difficulty dealing with her depression, so she sought treatment. Two years passed, and the family went to seek answers as to why she had not been released. The facility claimed she was still under treatment. When the family insisted on her immediate release, the hospital refused. The family sought assistance from the sheriff. Once the law was involved, the patient was found competent enough by the staff to leave the facility. It was then that the family learned the true reason for her extended stay. Evidently, she was a very good cook and had been working in that capacity for the two years of her confinement, without compensation. After all, without proper funding, staffing was a serious issue.

As the death toll rose at the facility, families were left with unanswered questions. They are unanswered to this day. A fire destroyed most of the documents, leaving most of the patients' death records unobtainable. Many of their bodies remain there, buried in unmarked graves, a consequence of poor upkeep and the condition of the cemetery.

Almost a century of care had passed by the time the facility closed. Thousands of patients and staff called the location home. Many came and went; others never saw the outside of the walls again. There are several theories on the cause of death of past residents. Electroshock therapy was used during that time, along with a new procedure known as a lobotomy. Eastern State was considered one of the leading psychiatric hospitals of

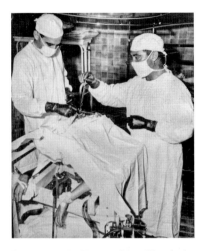

Surgery at the Eastern State Hospital.
Oklahoma Historical Society.

its day, and one of the first lobotomies in the United States was conducted there. It was also one of the locations used to test a new drug, Thorazine. It is still used today. Another experimental treatment was the use of high insulin doses on nondiabetic patients. The idea was to attempt to "shock" the patient's brain back to normalcy. This procedure failed, causing all five of the test subjects to slip into diabetic comas. Fortunately, medicines were available to help reverse the potentially deadly experiment.

With a lack of records and limited funding for research into the facility's medical history, the identities of many patients who died at the location are unknown. As mentioned earlier, many were buried in unmarked graves, and some bodies are said to be stacked two or three high. Perhaps this is why so many reports have been made about paranormal activity at the site. People report driving at night and seeing someone wandering down the street before they suddenly vanish. Lights are seen at night in some buildings at the facility when no electricity is found to be operating. Shadows have been reported moving across windowpanes, as if residents and staff continue to do their daily chores. Perhaps for many of the poor souls whose spirits remain, time has stood still, and they are trapped within the walls that held them so many years ago. Do some of these spirits seek answers or justice for an untimely death, or do they simply not realize that they are dead and don't know how to move on? Understanding what goes on inside someone else's mind is incomprehensible. Perhaps they continue to live in a loop of madness, not understanding the difference between life and death. Some patients were institutionalized merely because they suffered a momentary depression or were physically challenged but had full mental capacity and were at Eastern State Hospital due to a lack of resources. What would it have been like for them, being institutionalized alongside those suffering from severe mental illness or, worse, the criminally insane? The uncertainty and possible horror each patient faced is hard for us to understand. For all of these reasons, this location is at the top of the list of haunted places, and the land it stands on is forever tarnished with the blood of its former inhabitants. Today, the grounds, owned by the state, are

Eastern State Hospital abandoned site.

abandoned. Trespassing is strictly prohibited. For a paranormal investigator like myself, this location is considered the equivalent of the Ark of the Covenant. Fortunately, I have sense enough to avoid time in jail and a hefty fine. Even so, that is preferable to what could happen at such a dangerous location. If you happen to be driving down a dark country road south of Vinita and see a person wandering the highway, do not stop and offer them a ride. You might also want to take a quick look in the rearview mirror to make sure you left them behind and that they are not sitting in your back seat.

AUTHOR'S NOTE: EVEN TODAY, research and treatment in the field of mental health are not as advanced as desired. In many cases, funding is cut annually, leaving jails overcrowded with the mentally ill and staff not trained to handle situations. Budgets don't allow for the necessary training of staff. Take a stand for those who cannot stand up for themselves. It is important to fight for the necessary funding to treat and care for the mentally ill. They need a voice. Lend them yours.

5

CLAREMORE

The city of Claremore was named the county seat for Rogers County just after Oklahoma attained statehood in 1907. But Claremore's history began long before that. The town was named after an Osage leader, Chief Claremore, whose nearby village was destroyed in 1817 during the Battle of Claremore Mound. In 1874, when the area was still part of the Cherokee Nation's Indian Territory, the first post office was established. The first railroad reached the townsite in 1882, providing a better means of travel into Indian Territory and facilitating future land runs. In May 1903, Claremore was incorporated. With the discovery of healing mineral waters, the town began to flourish. In 1919, just two months after the end of World War I, a military academy was established in Claremore. It became Oklahoma's primary training grounds for the U.S. armed forces. It continued to operate for the next fifty-two years, training cadets who went on to fight in the nation's wars and military operations. Claremore has played a major role in the state's history, including being near the birthplace of actor Will Rogers, who often referred to the town as home, since most people could not pronounce the name *Oologah*, his actual birthplace. With a long history of military activity and the forced relocation of Native Americans, it's no wonder that Claremore has more than its fair share of ghostly activity. When one digs into the past, one often finds not only history, but also hidden skeletons longing to be found.

HAUNTED BELVIDERE MANSION

Nestled deep in the heart of Claremore, Oklahoma, sits a magnificent, three-story Victorian home. With its pointed turrets piercing the evening sky, this Gothic-style structure gives off an ominous presence. John M. Bayless started construction on the castle-like mansion in 1902 for his wife, Mary, and their seven children. Bayless was a wealthy businessman who became successful in the railroad and banking industries and as a land developer. He spared no expense in the building of his nine-thousand-square-foot home. With intricate details on every facet of the mansion, it took several years to complete. It was a labor of love, one he didn't see to completion. Just six months before the home was finished, Bayless suffered an attack of appendicitis and passed away just after his operation. His wife and children continued with the building of their family home and lived in it until 1919.

In the early 1920s, the mansion was converted into an apartment complex, and it remained in this capacity for many years. The property then passed through several hands until it was acquired by the Rogers County Historical Society, which returned it to its previous state. This architectural beauty offers visitors a step back in time to its glory days, filled with fine furniture from the period, beautiful art pieces and perhaps a little more.

Multiple witnesses have given accounts over the years of possible paranormal activity in Belvidere Mansion. Disembodied footsteps are often heard wandering the halls when no one else is there. Shadowy figures and full-bodied apparitions have also been reported in various locations. Even John Bayless has been rumored to roam the darkened hallways, despite his not having seen the completion of the home. John is not alone, it appears. Mary and some of their children have also been seen in the home over the years. The ghostly apparition of a young lady has been reported as well, though she doesn't seem to be a Bayless family member. It may be the spirit of a young woman who allegedly killed herself in the 1940s while residing in one of the apartments.

Whether or not one believes in the spirit world, we can all agree that this marvelous building has a dark past full of mystery and wonder. Visitors are lured to the home in the hopes of stepping into the past, when Oklahoma was facing a new world all its own. So the next time you find yourself traveling along Historic Route 66 in Claremore, stop and visit the old mansion. Grab a quick bite at the Pink House restaurant located inside Belvidere Mansion or take a tour. Perhaps join in a murder mystery. Just make sure the person you see is one of the actors or guests playing a part and not the spirit of someone from long ago, because you never know who or what you might run into at the Belvidere.

CLAREMORE INDIAN HOSPITAL

The Belvidere Mansion isn't the only location in Claremore rumored to be haunted. The Claremore Indian Hospital also has a haunted reputation. Its history may not be as long as that of the Belvidere, but it carries a dark past all its own. The hospital is rumored to be visited by the ghostly apparition of a woman in white. The woman, Wilma, a former employee at the hospital, met her death at the end of a knife wielded by someone she had once loved.

Wilma spent her life caring for patients in the very hospital where she would take her final breath. She was a nurse, working a daily shift. The beginning of her end began several months earlier. On July 15, 1979, she and her husband and other family members, including their grandchildren, were in their home near Claremore when her husband, Jesse, flew into a drunken rage. He claimed, "I am a murdering [bleeped] and could go get a gun and come back and kill all of you and get away with it because (a certain attorney) will get me off!" Immediately after, Wilma left the home and got an apartment in Claremore. On July 18, Jesse was served divorce papers. In the early morning of July 27, he was drinking in a local bar and told a waitress that he was having issues with his wife. Before he left, he called Wilma. He left the bar and went to a nearby hardware store, where he purchased a boning knife. He then went to her place of work. When Jesse reached the hospital, he asked where he could find her and was directed to a room where Wilma was working at the time. Muffled screams where heard coming from the room, and Jesse soon appeared with blood soaking his hands. Wilma was found slowly dying in a pool of her own blood, stabbed repeatedly by the knife Jesse had just purchased. Jesse was convicted of first-degree murder and sentenced to life in prison. Wilma's story doesn't end there. Over the years, several reports have been made by witnesses claiming to see Wilma's mournful specter continuing to walk the halls of the pediatric wing of the hospital. Perhaps her spirit continues to watch over the precious lives she once took such loving care of. For her sake, I hope she will one day find the peace that her soul truly deserves.

I Can Feel It Coming in the Air Tonight, oh Lord, oh Lord...

Admit it, if you were a child of the 1980s, you sang that Phil Collins lyric. I know I did. Being a nurse for the past twenty-five years, I can attest to the fact that we work a ton of hours. As a matter of fact, I can honestly say that most of my life has been spent on the job one way or another. But it appears that not only nurses can be married to their work. This ghostly encounter takes place at a college radio station at Rogers State College. The station, RSU Radio, also known as KRSC-FM 91.3, is run by student volunteers. But it's not a student who is rumored to haunt the halls. In 1989, a former program director died suddenly of a heart attack in the lobby of the old station. Over the next few years, several students reported seeing his spirit walking in the building and the nearby parking lot. In the 1990s, the building was demolished and a new one erected in another location on campus. But this didn't seem to end the ghostly encounters witnessed by the student body. Many people still claim to see his spirit walking the grounds where he once spent endless hours planning out the shows.

He's not the only one thought to walk the grounds of this college. At least two other spirits have been seen in various locations on campus. One spirit appears to be that of a young cadet rumored to have died during a hazing incident when the school was a military academy. He is often reported to be haunting the college TV station. Another specter seen on the grounds appears to be that of an elderly Native man. He walks the grounds, his path unknown. These are just three of the spirits rumored to haunt the halls and grounds of Rogers State College, but with the history of the area along this part of Route 66, I can only image what other spirits might tread here. The next time you find yourself traveling down this part of the route, turn your radio station to 91.3 FM. Perhaps you will hear a voice other than that of the DJ coming through your radio.

6

TULSA

I n the upper northeastern corner of Oklahoma is the second-largest city in the state. Tulsa originated in the 1820s, when the Creek Indians were forcefully removed from their ancestral homes in Georgia and Alabama and relocated to Indian Territory. Cattle ranching soon became a major industry in the area, leading to the arrival of ranchers, including one by the name of George Perryman. Arriving in Indian Territory in 1879, Perryman purchased a large parcel of land to develop his ranch. The ranch was so large that its original footprint is now the entire southern Tulsa area. In 1882, the railroad arrived, promoting the area to a city. In 1884, the first school was built, and by 1889, the city had become incorporated. In 1901, oil was discovered at Red Fork; in 1905, oil was found in Glenpool. Despite not having oil fields of its own, Tulsa encouraged oilmen to bring their business to the city and worked toward making it a welcoming place for large corporations. In the early 1900s, a fire destroyed half of the central business district. This led to the formation of the Tulsa Fire Department in 1905. The city continued to build and improve, and in 1912, the Hotel Tulsa opened its doors and soon earned the reputation of being the finest hotel in the Midwest. Not long after, Tulsa proclaimed itself the "Oil Capital of the World"—again, despite having no oil fields in the city limits. But it did have several petroleum refineries, and most of the famous oilmen of the day resided in Tulsa. Petroleum processing soon became a major part of the city's economy.

Left: Tulsa Route 66 welcome sign.

Opposite: Buck Atom's, Tulsa.

The Cosden Oil Refinery, located in Tulsa, was the largest independent oil refinery in the world at that time. With the oil fields booming, Tulsa boomed right along with them. The population grew, and new businesses began to pop up. Unfortunately, with growth and development came crime and murder. In the summer of 1921, Tulsa bore witness to its darkest time, an event that would scar Tulsa even to this day.

Greenwood, located in the historic district of Tulsa, was once the most prominent and concentrated African American district in the United States. Better known as Black Wall Street, it was a town within a town, providing services to the residents of the district. Many business owners became independently wealthy, owning new cars and homes and elevating their social status. This didn't sit well with many of the white residents of Tulsa. On Memorial Day weekend of 1921, Dick Rowland, a young African American, was accused of assaulting a young girl by the name of Sarah Page, an elevator operator in the building where he worked shining shoes. Rowland was arrested and placed in jail. Word soon spread that a white mob was planning to lynch Rowland. A group of seventy-five African American men, some armed with guns, arrived at the jail to offer protection and attempt to prevent the lynching. The sheriff assured the crowd that he had the situation under control and persuaded them to leave. The group was approached by

an elderly white man who demanded they hand over their guns. The men refused, and the elderly man attempted to forcefully disarm one of them. A single gunshot was fired, and this led to a larger exchange of gunfire. The group of African Americans ran back to their homes in Greenwood as word of potential violence began to spread like wildfire through the town.

A mob of white rioters assembled and headed to the Greenwood district. They invaded the district, killing men, looting stores and homes and setting fire to business establishments and homes. Millions of dollars in damage was inflicted on Black Wall Street, leaving almost ten thousand residents homeless. Those murdered during the massacre were buried in an unmarked mass grave, and the incident was wiped from history until 1996, seventy-five years after the massacre. A bipartisan group in the state legislature authorized the formation of the Oklahoma Commission to Study the Tulsa Race Riot. Its report stated that the city had conspired with the mob that ultimately ended in death and destruction. New laws were enacted requiring that schools teach about the history of the race riot. Special scholarships and funding have been set aside to aid the descendants of the victims of the riot. Research is underway in an attempt to locate the mass grave and to provide a proper burial for those killed and a location where their descendants can pay their respects. Today, Greenwood is once again booming, with many African American businesses dedicated to honoring those who perished while also trying to build a better life for themselves and their families.

With such a dark past, it's no wonder that Tulsa continues to be haunted by spirits. There are several locations around Tulsa rumored to be haunted. One is the Brady Theatre. Now known as the Tulsa Theater, it was built in 1914 and is located in the Tulsa Arts District. The building's name was officially changed in 2019, as the name *Brady* referred to a member of the local Ku Klux Klan. During the Tulsa Race Riots, the theater was used as a detention center for African American men rounded up by the National Guard. In the past century, the theater has played host to various events and musical acts. One of those who performed is said to haunt the theater to this day. In 1921, the Italian opera singer Enrico Caruso visited Tulsa to perform at the theater. After he returned home, he developed pleurisy, which would claim his life. His manager blamed his premature death on his trip to Tulsa,

Historic Tulsa Massacre site. *Oklahoma Historical Society.*

claiming that the famous singer acquired the disease while riding in an open carriage. Despite Caruso passing away in his home in Italy, the spirit of the singer is said to haunt the theater, forever laying the blame at the city's feet. He isn't the only spirit said to haunt the Tulsa Theater. The spirit of another man roams among the seats of the historic venue. The spirit is said to be that of a worker who fell to his death while doing repairs from the top of a tall ladder. Whether the person died in the theater or thousands of miles away, their spirit continues to haunt this old theater and possibly always will.

The Tulsa Theater isn't the only site rumored to be haunted in the Tulsa area. Two of its famous museums, the Gilcrease Museum and the Philbrook Museum, also lay claim to restless spirits wandering their hallways. The Gilcrease Museum, established in 1949, houses a collection related to the art, culture and history of North America. A Tulsa oilman and citizen of the Muscogee Creek Nation by the name of Thomas Gilcrease established the museum to exhibit works of art depicting the American West and archaeological artifacts dating back to as early as 12,000 BC. Gilcrease passed away in 1962, leaving the museum under the city's care. But it appears he continues to watch over the facility even after his death. Reports of paranormal activity include disembodied laughter, doors slamming, disembodied footsteps and even the appearance of Native American children playing in the gardens. With the museum containing so much history, one can't help but wonder how many spirits might haunt its grounds.

The Philbrook Museum of Art is also rumored to be haunted. The museum first opened its doors in October 1939, offering visitors an array of gardens to walk through extending more than twenty-five acres. The museum also houses over sixteen thousand objects and artworks focusing on American and Native American art as well as European art. Prior to its use as a museum, this Italian Renaissance villa was the private residence of Waite and Genevieve Phillips on its completion in 1927. The family lived there until 1938, when Waite Phillips announced that he would be gifting the seventy-two-room mansion and surrounding grounds as an art center for the city of Tulsa. Along with the gift of art, it seems Tulsa received a little something extra: a ghost. Guests report an ominous feeling while visiting the museum, and it seems that the eyes in various works of art follow visitors wherever they walk. Some even report seeing the heads on certain pieces slightly turn, watching as they walk by. Do spirits haunt this historic museum, or is it just an urban legion that continues to grow as more people visit in hopes of witnessing paranormal activity for themselves? The only way to know for sure is to take a trip to Tulsa and see this amazing museum

Tulsa Route 66.

for yourself. As you wander the magnificent halls, take in the beauty of the art on display, but make sure to keep your eyes open in case you are lucky enough to witness a bit of paranormal activity.

Tulsa, like Oklahoma City, seems to be bursting at the seams with paranormal activity. There is one more location I'd like to mention, one that is found along Historic Route 66. The story was shared with me by the general manager of Heirloom Rustic Ales, located at 2113 East Admiral Boulevard in Tulsa. The brewery offers a variety of twelve beers made in-house for visitors to enjoy in a fun and relaxing atmosphere. At times, though, the atmosphere takes on a different feeling, giving guests a taste of a different kind of spirit—one that refused to leave.

Jessica Hermann was gracious enough to share with me some of the paranormal activity that she and her staff have witnessed, as well as some of the history associated with the building. Prior to becoming a brewery house, the site served as a garage and auto shop. It is not known what might have taken place here, but some people speculate that a murder happened many years ago. The real history is unknown at this time, but what is certain is that the staff continues to witness paranormal activity. Guests and staff have reported feeling as if they are being watched by a set of unseen eyes. Jessica reports that her office appears to be colder than the rest of the building, no matter the time of year. Full glasses of beer have been seen flying off tables, as if someone is forcefully shoving them to the floor. So, if you're looking to quench your thirst with a cold brew and experience some spiritual activity, stop by Heirloom Rustic Ales and find out for yourself just what kind of spirits are on tap.

7

SAPULPA

Sapulpa, located about twelve miles southwest of Tulsa on Historic Route 66, is in Creek County and serves as the county seat. Around 1850, a full-blooded Lower Creek Native American, James Sapulpa, came to Indian Territory and established a trading post. In 1886, with the arrival of the railroad, a depot was built. James became friends with many of the railroad workers, and it was decided to name the station after him. It would be known as Sapulpa Station. Not long after this, a post office was built. The town became incorporated on March 31, 1898. A few years before incorporation, the Euchee Mission Boarding School was built to educate Native American children, or so was the claim. These boarding schools were established to force a new way of life and beliefs on the children, who were often forcefully removed from their homes and families to prevent them from retaining or learning their tribes' culture. For the first few decades, the population of Sapulpa rapidly grew, and with the discovery of oil and other natural resources in and around the area, the town began to flourish. As with most towns, the population fluctuated, depending on the economy. But like any other town, with prosperity came crime, and it appears that Sapulpa saw its fair share of it over the years.

Historic downtown Sapulpa offers many things to see and do. It has a small-town feel as you walk the streets, with several little shops and eateries to enjoy. The weekend we were there happened to be when the town was hosting a founder's celebration. One of the main streets was blocked off and occupied by tents offering crafts and delicious things to eat. Music

Euchee Indian School, Sapulpa. *Sapulpa Historical Museum.*

could be heard on the streets, and friends and families talked and enjoyed the activities. My dear friend Stacey and I were headed to a local restaurant to meet the rest of our group for a quick bite before heading to the night's investigation sites. Before arriving at our location, we stopped at one of vendor booths exhibiting information about their business. Stacie was chatting with the owners about their new bagel shop when I happened to notice the picture of a large historic building they were displaying. It just happened to be one of the buildings I had been drawn to several weeks before, when I had come to town to do some research. I inquired about the picture, and the owner informed me that it was the site of their business. I immediately asked her about the haunting associated with it. At first, she denied any ghostly activity, as most people would. For some, when they hear you talking about ghosts or hauntings, they look at you with a sideways glance, with the implication that you might be crazy. Well, they used to, anyway. Today, people are a little more open to sharing their experiences, which makes it easier for others to do the same.

When I explained to her who I was and my purpose for being there, she relaxed enough to share a few stories and experiences. The building they owned used to be the meeting lodge for the Independent Order of Odd Fellows (IOOF). Established in 1806 in New York City, this group consisted of members ranging from actors to boatbuilders. Over the years, lodges and chapters began to form across the United States, and in 1851, IOOF became the first national fraternity to accept both men and women. The only stipulation for membership was that the applicant was white. Many of its members belonged to the Ku Klux Klan. While researching their

Sapulpa Indian School students. *Sapulpa Historical Museum.*

building, the current owners were given copies of pictures showing a KKK meeting being held in the building—not just in the building, but upstairs in what would now be considered their living room, since the owners live above the shop. Much like the Masons, the IOOF had secretive rituals and rites they conducted during meetings. These practices were never spoken of or shared beyond the walls of the meeting places. If only those walls could talk. One mystery that could be solved is that of an old coffin found hidden in a secret room in the building. Finding a hidden coffin in any building would pique anyone's interest, but finding the skeletal remains of a small woman in the coffin would blow one's mind. Why would such a thing be hidden in an old lodge? Who was she, and why was she hidden there? These are questions I would love to find the answers for, should I ever be granted permission to investigate the site. Paranormal activity does occur from time to time we are told. Disembodied footsteps can often be heard. One can only image what else might be discovered in the secret passageways of the historic Odd Fellows lodge.

Several locations drew my interest around the town of Sapulpa. One such place is Crossroads Cookery. Located in one of the beautiful historic brick buildings lining Dewey Street, this restaurant offers an array of food choices, not to mention an amazing ice cream counter for those with a sweet tooth, like me. My team and I, along with Stacey and her team, were set to meet up that evening for a series of investigations in multiple locations around

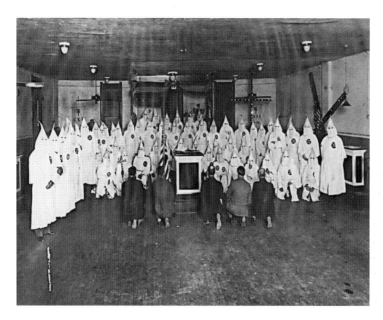

Ku Klux Klan meeting at the Odd Fellows building, Sapulpa. *Sapulpa Historical Museum.*

town. A few of us had decided to meet for dinner, and Stacey suggested the Crossroads. As we entered the building, it became obvious that this place had more to offer than just delicious sorbet. We were seated at a table just north of a long bar area where servers moved around, tending to their guests. I sat quietly, attempting to focus on the energy I was feeling within the dark walls. On a whim, I decided to walk over to the bar area and order a drink. A sudden image popped into my head, and I found myself blurting out to the bartender, "So who's the old cowboy spirit that wanders around up by the front door?" I caught a quick expression on his face as he responded, "We're not sure, but we often hear the sound of someone walking around there as well as on the stairs." I asked him if he knew what kind of activity occurred in or around the kitchen area, where a prankster spirit had been reported moving things or tossing them around. He said that he had been there only a few months and was seldom in the kitchen area but would ask around for me. He did say that upstairs always had a particular feel to it and confessed that there were several artifacts from various regions stored there. My group continued with our talk as we ate our dinner, preparing for the night ahead. As we left the restaurant with our bellies full and our minds spinning, a mental note was made to return to the Crossroads one day and, if we have time, perhaps reach out to the spirits that linger there. Hopefully, we will be able to discover their history and perhaps the reason they continue to live on in the walls of the Crossroads.

Left: Inside historic Newberry Building, Sapulpa. *Sapulpa Historical Museum.*

Below: Outside the historic Newberry Building, Sapulpa. *Sapulpa Historical Museum.*

Our next location was the one we had been anxiously waiting to investigate. Having visited the site the week before, we were confident that the activity we would experience would be well worth the wait. With two locations to investigate and two teams available for the research we decided to split up into groups and rotate during the night. Our second location was only a few blocks away, which made it easier for us to commute between the two. My team started off the evening investigating the museum first.

Sapulpa Historical Museum

Located at 100 East Lee Avenue in Sapulpa, this museum resides in a three-story brick building on the southwest corner of the street. Originally known as the Willis, this location played host to a series of businesses over the years. The first floor housed several businesses, including the Lee Ave Café, a newsstand, a jewelry store, a piano shop and a Maytag store. The third floor consisted of a ballroom and classrooms for a local business college. The second floor housed the old Lee Hotel, which operated there from 1910 to 1922. In 1922, the Young Women's Christian Association (YWCA) took over the second floor to offer living quarters to young women of Sapulpa and remained in business until 1968. It was in that year that the historical society was formed, but it had yet to find a permanent home for its museum. With the stipulation that the building be donated to a nonprofit organization, it was deeded to the newly formed historical society. In the late 1970s, the museum opened its doors to the public, offering visitors a glimpse into the town's history and helping to preserve items from the early years. Today, the museum houses various exhibits and items depicting different timelines and representing businesses throughout the years.

Like many other historic locations, this building has its own dark secrets. With years of human activities and emotions seeping into the bricks of the old building's walls, the past continues to live on here. During our visit, as the night progressed, we discovered just how much history remained.

We set up pieces of equipment in the front area of the museum. Several small rooms lined the entryway, each depicting a different scene or location from the town's early years. One of the rooms included a female mannequin and various pieces of clothing. I was drawn to the area and headed there with a few pieces of equipment on hand. The moment I crossed the threshold, a shift in energy could be felt. Something or someone was with me, despite me having entered alone. I called out to another member of the team to join me, to see if they too felt the energy shift. After I received confirmation that she felt the difference as well, we set up the equipment in the small closed space and began asking questions. We soon began to receive what appeared to be intelligent answers to our questions. The activity continued for several more minutes, and then another entity started to make itself known. This one was just beyond the wall, in an even smaller room directly behind the wall I had been leaning against. We were both drawn to a small safe standing near the back of the area. We placed an REM pod (an electronic device with a tall antenna that emits light and sound alarms should an entity touch

Sapulpa Historical Museum.

it or change the energy in its location) on top of the safe. We immediately began to get responses. We asked a series of questions there as well, using the device as a way for the spirit to answer. The entity made itself known and made sure that we knew it was not happy with our presence. This was its space and its safe, and we were not welcome.

We decided to continue with our investigation and headed to the second floor. I was curious to see what we might encounter there. Earlier that evening, I had experienced something that left me a little unnerved. People often ask me the scariest thing I have encountered or if I get scared doing what we do. In the past, there were times when I did get scared, but having done this as long as I have, it doesn't happen much anymore. You almost

Old Sapulpa Train Depot. *Sapulpa Historical Museum.*

become desensitized over time, so when I do find myself a little unnerved at a location, I tend to pay particular attention. This happened to be one of those locations. Earlier that evening, I was downstairs in the office with Rachel, the museum's curator, while she helped me locate some research material. I had sent my team to the upper floors to start the investigation without me, planning to join them shortly. One group returned while the other was still upstairs. I was told they were on the second floor, so I headed up to retrieve them. I was filming a live feed for Facebook as I went, and I am glad I did—or at least I am sure the Facebook live audience was, since one of those rare, unnerving moments was caught on camera for them. I exited the elevator into the small entryway, lit by a single light that did not extend far beyond the archway of the room. As I stepped beyond the light, I found myself engulfed in darkness. It wasn't just any darkness, but an eerie darkness, one that sends chills to the bone. I slowly walked down the long hallway, calling out for my team members and expecting someone to answer. But I was met only by silence. I continued on, thinking that perhaps they had not heard my first call. I once again tried to call out as I moved deeper into the darkness. Still no answer was heard. I knew someone was there, but it wasn't the people I set out to find. A chill started up my spine as I felt someone or something standing directly in front of me—something that my eyes could not quite see. I decided that this was not a place I wanted to be in alone.

I returned downstairs to rejoin the others and noticed that the other group had returned while I was away. I told them what I had encountered moments before, so we gathered our equipment and headed back upstairs to see if we could discover what it was that had unnerved me. We ended up at the very back of the hallway, just past a set of stairs that led to the floor below. Immediately, the equipment began to sound off all around us. I was sitting on the floor next to the stairwell with my back against the wall when

I felt a cold breeze. The equipment's alarms indicated the energy shift I had just felt. A coldness started to take over my right leg. It felt as if a small child had sat on my lap. I told the rest of the group what I was experiencing, and Sheila began to take pictures of the area where I reported the cold spot. We reviewed several of the photographs, and a foggy white haze could be seen floating just above the area where I reported feeling it.

The investigation continued, and soon our attention was drawn to the stairwell where we had set up a stand for trigger lights. The lights began to pulse and flash, indicating a nearby presence. Light sequences that had never been witnessed before began to emerge from the single stand of light. Thinking that the lights might be malfunctioning or that wiring on the floor was responsible, we gathered the other three stands and laid them in the same area. An electromagnetic field measuring (EFM) device was used to sweep the area to try to locate possible energy sources such as wiring, but none was found. Before long, all four stands of the trigger lights began to respond in various patterns. During this time, we had our ghost radio running, and we started receiving responses that appeared to be intelligent answers to our questions. Images began to form in my mind, and I asked if someone had hanged themselves from the banister. The curator said that she had not seen any articles about anyone hanging themselves there. We continued with our line of questioning. We received several responses pertaining to gambling, as well as a few other responses. But one response I found rather odd. It was the word *closet*. The word had come up not once but twice, so I jokingly asked if the spirit had "come out of the closet." The trigger lights began to light up all at once. Again, an image appeared in my mind, and I asked the curator if she knew of any deaths in the building—specifically, if anyone had committed suicide when the location was a hotel. It was then that the puzzle pieces began to fall into place. The curator suddenly remembered a story she had just come across about a local gambler who died in the hotel. He was known about town and liked to play pool. He was found dead with a suicide note next to him. It stated that he wished to be buried the way he was. During the preparation of the body for burial, the possible meaning behind the note was discovered. It was revealed that the person everyone presumed was a man was born a woman. The death was ruled a suicide on the evidence of the note, but to many people the wounds suggested otherwise. There were two stab wounds, one to the neck and a second to the chest. I can barely stand to stick my own finger with a needle, so I can't begin to understand how someone could drive a knife into their own chest or neck.

Staircase at the old Willis Building, currently the Sapulpa Museum. *Sapulpa Historical Museum.*

Time was passing quickly, and we had another location to investigate before the night was through. We decided to end there in hopes of returning to find out more answers about the gambler. We left the museum and headed over to the last stop for the night. We left the museum behind, but my mind was plagued with a question that could not be so easily forgotten. Did this person truly commit suicide, or was he a victim of an unsolved murder? Could that be why the spirit has not passed on? Could it simply be waiting for the truth to be told so it can finally rest in peace? I look forward to the day we return to the museum to see if we can uncover the truth that might be hidden within the walls of the old hotel. Restless spirits still wander the halls, looking for something they might have been denied so many years before: justice.

Bearded Lady

Located just a few blocks from the museum is a small beauty shop, the Bearded Lady. When we arrived at the shop, the location seemed to me small in size. But when we entered, I found it anything but small. Like many buildings erected in the early years of statehood, this one had a small front facing the street but extended much farther behind, making it much larger in size than indicated from outside. The first room houses various barber chairs, even an antique one propped up in the back corner, reminding us of the chairs that used to greet patrons many years ago. We were greeted by the owners, a very pleasant couple who welcomed us to their establishment. They began to share their experiences during their time at this location. They reported items seemingly moving on their own and an incident in which a boy visiting the shop day was seen holding a conversation with someone sitting in the antique chair—someone only he could see.

After a quick visit and a walk through the building, we set up our equipment and turned down the lights to begin our investigation. Intelligent responses were soon provided to our questions, and once again the equipment began to respond in various spots in the building. Words began to form a storyline, piecing together some of the history associated with this location. An image of a man slumped against the wall, the veil of death clouding his eyes, started to form in my mind. Bloodstains soaked his shirt as a bullet wound began to emerge in the vision before me. I asked the owner if she was aware of any shootouts happening during Prohibition, as many of our responses pertained to bootlegging and the law. She said that she was not aware of all of the building's history, but she did tell us of a bullet hole in the glass by the front door. Images continued to form in my mind, as if I was watching a movie—but I was sitting in the middle of the shop.

When we concluded our investigation, we returned to the museum to finish gathering up our things and to meet the rest of the team. The images I had just seen weighed heavily on my mind, so once again I turned to Rachel for possible answers. I asked her if she knew any history about the site of the Bearded Lady or any shootouts between law enforcement and bootleggers. She shared with me the story of a local lawman who was not only involved in a shootout with bootleggers but was also guilty of being one himself. He was charged and found guilty but was only suspended for a few days, then returned to work without further punishment. When I returned home, I continued to research that location, hoping to find something more to add to what I had experienced that night. A few weeks later, I discovered what I had been searching for. An article I located in an old newspaper spoke of a group of local lawmen who had engaged in a gunfight with bootleggers in front of a small shop next to an empty lot just a block from the corner of Main Street, historic Route 66. For these spirits, it appears they continue in death as they did in life, only now they will live on forever as spirits of Route 66.

Law Offices of Sapulpa

Two other haunted locations we investigated during my previous trip to Sapulpa were two law offices. One was located on Route 66, and the other was just a few blocks away. With Sapulpa being the county seat, a lawyer's office would be easy to find. But what about a lawyer who shares his office with aspects of Sapulpa's long-forgotten past? One such space is the Young Law Office. John Young, the current resident and an attorney in the building at Second North Main Street, a corner block on Route 66, is no stranger to Sapulpa. Born and raised here, he continues to call Sapulpa home. He comes from a long line of lawyers. His grandfather moved his family to this area many years ago at the beginning of his career. He then raised his son to follow in his footsteps, and this carried on to John and his children. The Youngs took over ownership of the current building in the 1950s after a large fire threatened their downtown location. In one night, they gathered all their files and began their evacuation to the current location, a site they would inhabit for the next seventy years. The building predates their time here, and in all of those years the building has played host to a variety of businesses—some legal and some maybe not so legal. Not everything that occurs in some buildings is documented, and for good reason it seems. This building may be one of those locations.

John Young, previously a lieutenant colonel in the United States Marine Corps, highly decorated and well educated, greeted us at the door and welcomed us into his historic building. As we sat and spoke about his family's history, John shared with us what history he knew of the building since the time his family took ownership of it. He took us upstairs to the area that has been reported to have activity. A paranormal team had visited the building in the past and conducted an investigation. It reported finding evidence to support a claim of the building's haunting. Stacey Price and I began our own investigation by setting up pieces of equipment in the largest open area upstairs. It had once served as a meeting place for a small church group but now sat empty except for a few pieces of furniture scattered around the room. Toward the front of the building, a small curved window overlooks the street below, its window encased in aged wood whose paint is slowly splintering away. As I stood at the window, gazing down at the pavement, I felt as if I was looking through someone else's eyes—the eyes of a young woman, a woman filled with despair and anguish. A sadness came over me, and it felt as if my heart had suddenly shattered into a million pieces. I shared with Stacey what I had just felt, and we placed some of our equipment around the location. Moments later, it appeared that we had contacted a spirit, that of a young lady. We watched as the equipment responded to our questions. We were ecstatic that we were able to make contact. Since our time was limited that evening and we had one more location to visit, we asked the spirit if there was anything else it wanted us to know. A large thump was felt, causing me and Stacey to lock eyes. It felt as if a large object had hit the floor, an object heavy enough to shake the entire building. We received our answer. We plan to return to this location in the future to see if we can discover the identity of the young lady who stands by the window, gazing out with such a heavy heart. Perhaps one day she can find peace and leave her heartache behind on Historic Route 66.

Just two blocks away is another law office that seems to be haunted by some of Sapulpa's long-forgotten residents. The Creek County Law Office, located at 101 East Lee Avenue, is in an old building that has played host to an array of businesses, including a dental office and a tire shop. The lawyers and staff there have been experiencing paranormal activity for some time and were kind enough to invite us in to investigate. As it was at the Young Law Office, the activity started almost immediately for us. Equipment was set up around the rooms and hallways, and Stacey and I split up. Still able to hear each other should one of us call out, we began our questioning. I was sitting in a high-back chair when I suddenly heard what sounded like footsteps running above my head. I called out to Stacey to ask if anyone was upstairs. She informed me that there was no upstairs, that this was a single-story building, a fact I had forgotten. I asked, if it was a spirit I heard, if it could do that again. I immediately heard the running footsteps again, only this time they sounded as if they were coming from the wall less than one foot from me. Luckily, I had been shooting video at the time and was able to catch the sounds on my recording. Stacey informed me that one of the reports of activity by the staff was the sound of disembodied footsteps running down the hallways. So what I had just heard had been witnessed before.

We continued with our investigation, receiving several responses to our questions. The spirits used the trip wires on command to answer. Knowing we were still extremely limited with time, we decided to do a quick electronic voice phenomenon (EVP) session in one of the back rooms at the end of the hallway. We asked a series of questions, and we were able to obtain responses on our audio device. We concluded the investigation for the night, but it left us asking more questions than before. Just who were these spirits that resided in this office? Was it even the office from which they originated? Attached to the building, separated by a brick wall, is a location that houses an organization that has other known haunted sites around the state. It is from this organization's location in Guthrie that I had obtained one of the best full-body apparition photographs many years ago. The building belongs to the American Legion. In the past, I have witnessed hauntings in many of its Oklahoma lodges. We plan on returning to the Creek County office and hope to visit the American Legion hall as well to see if we can discover which building the spirit belongs to. Or maybe it's a wandering spirit that moves through various buildings in Sapulpa's historic downtown and maybe also continues to haunt Historic Route 66.

8
KELLYVILLE

GHOST TRAIN

It was an early Friday afternoon, September 28, 1917, when passenger train no. 407 of the St. Louis–San Francisco Railway traveled along the tracks toward Sapulpa, Oklahoma. The steel engine screamed onward as the steam billowed from its smokestack. The engine was pulling a long row of wooden passenger cars in its wake. As the passengers chatted among themselves, many eagerly awaited the excitement of the weekend ahead. Many of them were on the way to a football game in one of the towns, but they would never arrive.

The passenger train had pulled over just a few miles back to allow another train to pass. A troop train had just returned from Fort Sill, where it had transported a group of soldiers who were preparing to ship out to fight in World War I. The engineer of the passenger train had received orders to pull to the side to allow the troop train to pass, and he did as instructed. Unfortunately, the orders weren't clear. Once the military train had passed, the passenger train resumed its route, unaware that a second train was coming toward it. That train was moving at full speed. The engineer of the passenger train realized his fatal mistake too late. Reports indicate that both trains were going full speed when they collided just two miles west of Kellyville at the Polecat Creek railway bridge. When the engineers of both locomotives saw the impending doom, they and the firemen in the

Above: Train wreck, Kellyville, 1917. *Sapulpa Historical Museum.*

Left: Train wreck site, Kellyville, 1917.

engines jumped from their respective trains. The wooden passenger cars splintered and snapped on impact. The mail car and the smoker were sent barreling into the Jim Crow car, where most of the fatalities occurred. Due to segregation laws, the Jim Crow car was designated for African Americans. Their death toll exceeded all other fatalities on the train.

The scene was described as one of pure horror. People involved in the cleanup of the site reported having to carry baskets of body parts that had become dismembered during the collision. Bodies were found cut in two, with lower halves still in seats and torsos ripped away. Most of the bodies were discovered under the wreckage of the mail car, which had sheared off the top of one of the passenger cars. Passengers' moans and screams could

Train wreck site today.

be heard as mutilated and injured survivors tried to crawl out from under the wreckage. Thirty-two passengers died that day; more than fifty were injured. It was the deadliest train accident in Oklahoma history. Due to the severity of the wreckage, laws pertaining to the construction of passenger cars were changed. The use of wood in their construction was prohibited. The old metal bridge can still be seen today, visible near the modern bridge on 66 that runs alongside the old railway tracks along Polecat Creek. Many travelers pass by the old bridge unaware of its significance or the tragedy that took place there over a century ago. A few houses can be seen scattered along the road to the side of the tracks, leaving one to wonder if the spirits of the victims continue to walk along the old rails, perhaps lost in a loop of time, unaware of their own deaths, since their lives were taken so suddenly. Or perhaps they continue to ride the rails in a train that will reach its destination on tracks running alongside Historic Route 66.

9

BRISTOW

ounded in 1898 with the arrival of the railroad and the establishment of a post office, Bristow began to blossom and grow. Located in Creek County, Bristow hoped to be named the county seat, but after a series of elections, Sapulpa won that privilege, leaving a bitter taste in the mouths of many residents. Determined to make Bristow a "first-rate" town, they set out to do just that. In 1923, a beautiful red-brick depot was built to welcome new arrivals, and in 1925, one of Oklahoma's first radio stations, KFRU, owned by millionaire E.H. Rolleston, filled the airways, bringing new life to the town. Residents soon welcomed the opening of Route 66, which ran through the heart of Bristow. Businesses have come and gone over the years, as have travelers. Since Route 66 was decommissioned, people don't seem to find their way to this sleepy little town very often. But unlike so many other small towns located along the route, Bristow has survived. It may not be considered one of the ghost towns on 66, but it does lay claim to ghosts. One haunted location is the historic Frisco Depot. The passenger trains that once visited Bristow daily are no longer seen, but their history lives on. The depot now houses the Bristow Historical Museum—and the ghost, which residents like to call Charlie. Its spirit has been reported to be felt around the building and, for some, has been seen. He offers no malice and causes no harm. To residents, he's simply Charlie. No one claims to know the identity of the residing spirit, though some have speculated. I often wonder how people come up with the names they give ghostly visitors, then I discovered an interesting bit of history during my

Bristow.

research. When the first post office opened in 1898, the postmaster was Charles C. Crane. Could this be the famous Charlie who currently haunts the old depot? With mail deliveries arriving and departing daily from the train station in the past, it certainly makes sense. Crane would have visited the depot often. Perhaps even after death Charlie continues with his work. Neither rain, nor snow and perhaps not even death can keep a U.S. Postal Service worker from delivering the mail.

Another Bristow location rumored to be haunted is a quick stop at the corner of Highway 48 and Route 66. Former employees have reported various types of paranormal encounters over the years. Activity has ranged from lights turned off and on by unseen hands, unexplained noises and objects being tossed at employees from across the room. Others have reported seeing the ghostly apparition of a young woman staring out the window onto the road. Many claim it is the spirit of a young woman who was hit by a truck while walking along Route 66—yet another life destined to forever roam the historic highway.

10

STROUD

THE HELL-RAISING TOWN

Named after James Stroud, a local trader, the town of Stroud soon became well known for more than just trading. Founded in 1892, Stroud served as a stopping place for many travelers and cowboys seeking to quench their thirst after a long trip along the dusty trails of Oklahoma. With Stroud's ability to sell whiskey and its border with the "dry" Indian Territory, it became a hot spot for cowboys and outlaws alike. As its population grew and more businesses opened, more travelers arrived. With nine saloons, Stroud took on a new nickname: the "Hell-Raising Town." Whiskey flowed freely, and for a few extra dollars, a lonely cowboy could find some company to pass the time. The population continued to grow until Oklahoma forced a ban on the sale of alcohol. The population of Stroud started to decrease, but despite the state's mandatory dry spell, the city's wild days were far from over. The Wild West still thrived in Stroud. In 1915, it became forever linked to the notorious outlaw Henry Starr. Along with six other men, Starr devised a plan to rob two Stroud banks simultaneously. Their attempt at a double daylight robbery proved disastrous for Starr. News spread quickly about the robberies, and citizens took up arms to defend their town. Starr and another outlaw, Lewis Estes, were shot and captured while trying to escape. Starr was tried, convicted, sentenced to prison and transferred to the Oklahoma State Prison in McAlester. He served four years and then was paroled, but even his time behind bars could not keep him from a life of crime. He attempted another bank robbery in 1921 in Harrison, Arkansas. He did not walk away from this one.

Left: Old Bar, Stroud.

Opposite: Old Motor Inn, Stroud.

Stroud's population fluctuated with the rise and fall of the economy. It became once again linked to a famous name when Route 66 was run through the heart of town. This brought a new era of travelers that continued for almost a century. Stroud lays claim to several historic locations and stops on the route. From the Skyline Motel to the Joseph Carpenter House—the oldest and best-preserved prairie house in Stroud—the town has many special places to offer the traveler. One place tends to stand out a little more than the others. Made nationally known by a chance visit from a Pixar production crew while it was traveling the route for research, the Rock Café earned a name for itself and put Stroud on the map once again.

Construction of the Rock Café began in 1936 by a local businessman, Roy Rieves. It was built by hand using refurbished sandstones removed from the old road while the new one was being paved. It took three years to complete the café, and in August 1939, the doors opened to welcome its first guest. Thelma Hollows oversaw the business. Soon, the eatery thrived as travelers

took to the road, and when it was added as a stop for the Greyhound bus company, business remained steady for many years. Several others managed the restaurant through the years, but for one new manager, her shift might have never ended. Mamie Mayfield took over running the café in 1959, keeping it open twenty-four hours a day. Buses arrived twice a day, filled with passengers from all walks of life. Some were on the way to visit family or friends; some were soldiers shipping out during World War II or returning home from a tour of duty. For decades, the Rock Café served guests by the thousands, but with the decommissioning of Route 66 and the construction of the Turner Turnpike, Rock Café began to feel the pinch of progress. Travelers opted for other routes, leaving the sleepy town to slowly fade from history. In 1983, the café closed its doors, but not for long. In 1993, a new owner made her mark. She brought life back to the Rock Café, reestablishing its rightful place on Historic Route 66.

Dawn Welch, along with her husband, her kids and close friends, began to renovate the café, mixing history with a unique twist. There was a new campaign to preserve and reestablish Route 66, and the café found itself playing a significant role in maintaining and preserving the highway's history. In 1999, the café saw a drop in commerce as an F2–F3 tornado touched down near Interstate 44 / Route 66. Stroud took a direct hit, and multiple buildings and businesses in the area were destroyed. This caused the loss of eight hundred jobs in a town of just under 3,200 residents. Many of those businesses did not return.

Times were tough. The café struggled, but its doors remained open. Around 2001, a crew from the Pixar animated movie *Cars* was traveling along the route doing research for the upcoming production when they happened to come across the Rock Café. The quirky personalities of Dawn and her staff caught the eyes of the crew. One of the movie's main characters would be fashioned after Dawn herself. The blue car known as "Sally" was inspired by Dawn, and this added a special attraction for Route 66 enthusiasts. Unfortunately, the café had to endure another disaster less than ten years later. This one did more damage requiring more time to fix. A massive fire engulfed the small café, gutting the building and causing extensive damage. Rebuilding took a year. Particular care was needed for the establishment to maintain its listing in the National Register of Historic Places. Once again, the Rock Café persevered. Today, it continues to serve delicious food prepared by Dawn and her staff. Whether the visitors are friends, neighbors or travelers driving along the route, the staff prides itself on treating everyone like family. Many who visit the café return often; some visitors never choose to leave!

The staff has come to know one spirit pretty well, one they acknowledge as "Mamie." There have been many strange reports and individual experiences by staff members over the years. Doors will often open or close by themselves. Paper-towel dispensers go off as if motioned by an unseen hand, leaving a pile of unraveled towels scattered on the floor. Despite every effort to re-create this anomaly, no explanation has ever been found. Disembodied footsteps are heard throughout the building when no other staff member or guest is present. The most unsettling activity is when objects start falling off the walls, but the regular staff tends to brush it off, believing it to be Mamie's way of making her presence known. It is said that she genuinely loved this place, and from what I have heard, she was loved in return. Could it be Mamie who haunts the café, or is it another wandering spirit of a former employee? Perhaps it is the spirit of someone who lost their life nearby. Maybe it's the spirit of a motorist or hitchhiker whose life was cut short on the winding roads of Route 66 and who continues to seek solace at the familiar café they may have visited so many years ago. Whatever it is that haunts the Rock Café appears to pose no threat to Dawn and her crew. In return, they acknowledge and greet them like they are family stopping in to grab a bite.

11
CHANDLER

stablished just six days after the land run of 1891, Chandler serves as the county seat for Lincoln County. Named after the assistant secretary of the interior, Judge George Chandler, the town has persevered. A devastating event nearly destroyed the town just six years after it was established. On March 30, 1897, a tornado struck Chandler, causing massive damage and claiming the lives of fourteen people. Hundreds more were injured. Despite the loss, the residents of Chandler held strong and started to rebuild. Buildings were reinforced to withstand the harsh Oklahoma winds; many of those structures still stand today, bearing witness to the strength of the people who built them. One of these historic buildings stands at 719 Manvel Avenue and currently houses the Lincoln County Historical Society and the Museum of Pioneer History.

Built in 1897–98, the Mascho-Murphy Building was erected by pioneer grocer A.E. Mascho to house his store on the site where a previous building had been destroyed. The new building stood strong and served as a grocery store until the mid-1970s, when it closed to make way for the historical society. It obtained the building for its museum, which is still there today. Various objects and exhibits are on display on the building's multiple levels. One exhibit features items related to one of Chandler's most well-known residents, the infamous lawman William "Bill" Tilghman. Like most museums, this location not only contains the history of the past but also houses spirits from the past.

Historic Chandler. *Museum of Pioneer History, Chandler, Oklahoma.*

Museum of Pioneer History, Chandler.

Sightings and experiences have been reported over the years. From disembodied laughter to objects moving on their own, paranormal activity seems to thrive within the mortar of this museum. Several paranormal teams have been in to investigate, all walking away with stories of their own while at the site. I reached out to a local paranormal investigator and friend, Bryan Herring, who was happy to share with me a few of the experiences he and others have had. He also shared how actors participating in a haunted house attraction at the museum had their own run-ins with the spirits. Shadow figures have been seen wandering the halls, and the sounds of things moving around are heard coming from the upstairs area when no one else is present. One team reported witnessing a heavy file cabinet drawer shutting on its own. When I visited the museum with my husband for research for this book, this old building definitely had a strange feeling to it. I was particularly drawn an old mirror adorning the wall at the top of the first stairwell. I stared at it for a long time, waiting to see if anything would manifest for me. I wasn't lucky that day, but when I did inquire about it, my feelings were confirmed. That area had been a paranormal hot spot for others in the past. I was drawn to the upstairs area, where I felt the presence of a nurse. The staff led me to the area where various nursing memorabilia is located, and I knew this was the area she had been from. Unfortunately, fully investigating the museum that day was not a possibility, since I had not brought any tools and no teammates came along. Had the chance presented itself, I'm positive that we would have encountered amazing activity. I settled for the tour and left knowing that this museum not only offered its guests a trip back into the town's history but also a chance to meet some of its past residents while walking the hallways.

The museum is not the only building rumored to be haunted in Chandler. Just one block away sits a quaint little (well, perhaps not so little) establishment, Manvel Avenue Coffee. We arrived just as the owner was closing the shop, but when I explained why I was there, he graciously invited us in. We sat and chatted for a bit, then I began to ask him questions about his location. He shared with us some of the building's past, from the moment the tornado tore the previous building from its foundation to another incident that claimed a building by fire. The current structure was built around 1908 and sits on top of the remains of the previous buildings. With the building comprising multiple levels, several businesses have occupied it over the years. Upstairs used to house a doctor's office and apartments prior to the 1950s, as well as another store and a jewelry store at one point. Steven Conway, the current owner, has been at this location for four years. He and other staff

Old mirror at the Pioneer Museum, Chandler.

have witnessed paranormal activity. Activity is reported happening toward the back of the shop, where knocking sounds are often heard, along with pounding on doors, lights going off and on by themselves, things falling off walls and shelves and even a paper towel dispenser operating on its own, leaving a mess for the staff to clean up. Motion sensors are set off, and some people have even witnessed the disembodied voice of a woman whom they have named Lily, as that name was found scratched into an old windowpane upstairs. Despite so many people witnessing paranormal activity over the years, no one claims to know the identity of the spirit or how many may linger there. The next time you feel like having a savory cup of coffee, take a trip to Chandler and stop in at Manvel Avenue Coffee. You might catch a glimpse of one of the resident ghosts, making the trip really worthwhile.

Historic Downtown Chandler. *Museum of Pioneer History, Chandler, Oklahoma.*

Manvel Avenue Coffee Company, Chandler.

Old Army, Route 66 Interpretive Center, Chandler.

The last location I want to mention is not for the faint of heart. It assumes a much darker nature. It is found just outside of town in an old cemetery. Bryan Herring and his team visited its location more than once. During one visit, they encountered a presence none of them were likely to forget. The New Zion Cemetery is just east of town. The team collected evidence from various investigations, including EVPs, sightings of shadow figures and recordings of growls via their digital video recorder (DVR) system. One night, the cemetery appeared to evoke a darker feeling than ever before. The team took multiple photos and audio recordings that night. During their review, they noticed a dark shadow figure lingering in one of the buildings nearby. They also discovered several "Class A" EVPs (very clear voices in which investigators can understand exactly what was being said) that sounded sinister in tone. This finding verified to the team what they had felt during the investigation, leading them to believe that something very dark resides at the cemetery, something that does not welcome intruders. The team has not been back at night to investigate since then, not out of fear but out of respect for the "No Trespassing" signs now posted on the cemetery gates. If you choose to visit the site during daytime hours, remember to be polite and try not to disrespect those who reside there. The last thing you want is for something to follow you home. If you happen to hear a growl during your visit, say your prayers and find your way out. Leave the spirit alone to reside at the New Zion Cemetery along Historic Route 66.

12

EDMOND

UNIVERSITY OF CENTRAL OKLAHOMA

Edmond's history began about the mid-1880s with the arrival of the Atchison, Topeka and Santa Fe Railway. First named The Summit and functioning as a water and coal station for the railroad, the station gained its new name in honor of freight agent Edmond Burdick. The area kept the name and adapted it to new town that began to grow around the station. As the town grew, so did businesses in the area. In 1891, the Territorial Normal School was built, offering classes to train new teachers desperately needed for the territory and its ever-growing population. The school changed its name several times over the next few years until a permanent name was adopted, one that survives to this day: the University of Central Oklahoma (UCO).

The first building to house the school was erected in 1893 and is known as the Old North Tower. This three-story, red-brick building houses a large-faced clock in the center tower. The long front hall extends the length of the old building; a shorter hall is located on either side of the structure. A building with a history of more than 130 years would be expected to see reports of paranormal activity. The most well-known spirit said to linger in the halls is that of the first president of the school, Richard Thatcher. Students and staff have reported seeing a ghostly figure of a man dressed in an old suit and a derby, one that Thatcher was known to wear. He is often

Old North at UCO, Edmond.

reported lingering around the clock area on the upper floors, looking out over the campus, as if he continues to watch over the school. His isn't the only spirit reported in the old building. A female teacher dressed in turn-of-the-century attire is also seen wandering the halls, primarily on the south end of the upper floors. A few years ago, I was asked to visit the campus to give a TED Talk to some of the students about paranormal research and for my team to lead an investigation through some of the college's buildings as a fun Halloween event.

The Old North Building was one of the sites we were assigned to investigate. The energy was palpable as we entered the structure and began to walk its halls. My investigators and I led a group of students to a room on the third floor, and we set up equipment around the room. We soon began to gather evidence needed to prove the existence of spirits. Various spirits seemed to respond to our line of questioning, but none as disturbing as that of a young woman who appeared to have committed suicide. She said that she had jumped to her death from the roof of the old building many years ago. Her anguish could be felt by many in the room; some began to tear up as her story unfolded. We asked the young woman why she had not moved on and why she lingered within the walls of Old North. She replied that she was afraid to move forward, unaware of what might await her in the afterlife, as she had chosen to take her own life. As we closed our session, we encouraged her to move on in the hopes of finding happiness and loved ones. We have not returned to the location since then to see if she did indeed move on, but we hope she found the happiness she was unable to attain while alive.

Another building rumored to be haunted is Mitchell Hall Theatre. Built in 1926, it was named after Central Oklahoma's president at the time, John G. Mitchell. The old building is said to be haunted by a maintenance worker who fell to his death during a production of a Thornton Wilder play in the 1940s. Strange things began to happen after his death. Reports surfaced of objects moving around the theater by unseen hands and doors seeming to open and close by themselves. Some students have reported seeing a man sitting in various sections of the theater's seating area. Pebbles that seem to appear out of nowhere have been tossed at students. The maintenance man's name is not known, but since he perished during a Thornton Wilder production, the students have named the spirit Thornton. To this day, when a student witnesses any type of paranormal activity, they say, "Oh, that's just old man Thornton letting us know he's still around." So the next time you visit Mitchell Hall Theatre to attend a production, you might end up seeing a little extra if you keep your eyes open. Perhaps Thornton will put on a performance of his own just for you.

Like most college campuses, UCO seems to play host to multiple spirits. A third building housing spirits is the old chapel, located near the middle of campus. This building is unique in many ways. It was designed and created almost entirely by the students and staff. Named the Y-Chapel of Song, its fourteen glass-stained windows depict themes of various religious songs sung at the time. Art students designed, fired and assembled the stained glass. With a lack of government funding to build the chapel, Dr. Jessie Newby Ray, PhD, a professor at the university, began a fundraising effort to obtain the means to build this student chapel. In 1948, construction began. With the help of students, facility and staff, the chapel was completed in April 1949. It served as a small meeting place for religious groups and for students seeking solitude. During the Vietnam War, the chapel was used to conduct funeral services, and this left an impact on the building's history.

During our investigation, some of the activity we witnessed referred to that fraught time in U.S. history, leaving its fingerprint and its spirits within the chapel's walls. The chapel also appears to retain history from racial strife and riots associated with the 1960s, when segregation once again reared its ugly head among students on campus. My team and I have been able to investigate this location twice, and with each investigation, similar evidence leads us to believe that the information we received about the riots and Vietnam are likely true. With our equipment registering responses, as well as EVPs we obtained, we feel that there is some legitimacy to the claims of paranormal activity in the chapel. Our most shocking piece of evidence is the opening and slamming of a heavy door on the south side of the building. The door was checked prior to the investigation and found to be locked. During our questioning, we asked for a sign that a spirit was among us. We received an answer when the locked door swung open and then slammed shut, startling everyone present. The spirits of the chapel may possess enough energy to slam the doors, but they don't have the status as the most sinister sprits on the campus grounds. That title belongs to the spirits of Murdaugh Hall. The building has a long history of reported evil within its walls.

Built in 1937, Murdaugh Hall, named in honor of the university's fourth president, Edmund Murdaugh, is in the heart of campus and serves as a student residence hall. The building is rumored to contain a series of tunnels that run deep beneath the campus and descend to an underground world where monsters reside. Legend has it that students who have gone into the basement area to do their laundry have heard strange noises, monster-like and frightening. Various holes mysteriously appear, and strange markings have often been seen. Students who have been reported missing were last seen entering the basement area; many believe they entered the labyrinth of passages, lost forever and unable to find their way back. We were able to access the basement, but we were not allowed to take students inside. The basement evokes an eerie doom and takes on a dark energy all its own. Dirt-filled crawl spaces extend in various directions, and smaller chambers can be found within larger rooms below. With the eerie darkness, it is easy to see how so many students could believe in the legends surrounding this location. It's not a place I would want to venture into alone on a dark night. It's places like this that give rise to dark tales, leading to nightmares for anyone brave enough to venture into the dark, forbidding space. Many enter, but not all return.

RIGHT-OF-WAY GRAVES

Located just west of UCO are the graves of two men. Frank Mosier and Willie Davis were crew members of the Southern Kansas Railroad, assigned to lay tracks through present-day Edmond. It was September 17, 1886. The weather was hot, and the two men's tempers were even hotter. A fight erupted between them due to causes unknown. The disagreement ended with both men dead. The two railroad employees were buried beside each other, their graves placed on the west side of the railroad right-of-way. Their bodies remain there to this day. A cross was placed at the graves at the time of burial. Years later, a red-granite marker was placed by the Oklahoma Historical Society to mark it as a historical site. For years, the graves were tended to by Santa Fe Railroad workmen, but due to budget restraints, the railway company ceased caring for the graves. Weather, time and vandalism have left them in poor states of repair, but the cross and marker remain.

EDMOND RAILYARD

Through the years, many people have perished along the railways of Oklahoma. Such tragic deaths and the energy surging through the iron tracks make for perfect conditions for ghostly activity. Add in buildings with historic significance located along a historic highway, and you have the makings of spooky attractions with no need for plastic props. This confluence of circumstances created the haunted location at the Edmond Railyard. The railyard's current appearance differs dramatically from that in the early years of statehood. Despite changes to its appearance, one aspect of the railyard remains the same: its ghostly inhabitants. The site's various businesses are housed in one general area, with large garage doors located at either side of the building that can be raised, creating an open

Historic Edmond
Railway, Edmond.
Oklahoma Historical Society.

space for visitors to wander from shop to shop. Multiple eateries, an ice-cream shop and even a wine bar can be found here. There is something for everyone—even a ghost or two.

One of the shops is no stranger to the railyard's paranormal activity. Michelle Spurlock, the owner of Blue J's Rockin' Grill, knows of a ghost that haunts the establishment. She has been a witness on multiple occasions to ghostly activities. She believes she may have figured out the identities of two of the spirits residing there. One of the spirits has even presented itself as a full-body apparition. Witnesses say he appears wearing a brown suit in the style of the early 1900s and a brown derby. John Stein, who resided at this location, was known to wear the same style of clothing, leaving many to speculate that this spirit may indeed be Stein. Another spirit often seen here is that of a woman. She appears to be from the same period and is believed to be John's wife, Cordilla. Witnesses have reported hearing a woman talking when no one else is there. Another spirit, that of a Native American girl, has been seen running around the area. She appears to be under the age of five; her identity and cause of death is unknown. In the wine bar, the spirit of a middle-aged man wearing a business suit and smoking a cigar is felt to be present in the private lounge located just above the bar. The room's wall is constructed of glass, allowing one to look out over the main floor and into the breezeway of the building. This spirit gives the impression that he is a wealthy man of business, surveying the activity below. One possibility for the cause of paranormal activity is the tragic death of a homeless man several years before. His lifeless body was found on the nearby tracks, a victim of a train accident. Whatever the identities of these spirits, they seem to feel at home in the railyard, and it seems they don't wish to leave. The next time you find yourself craving a burger or some amazing fries, head over to Blue J's Rockin' Grill. Pull up a chair, grab a bite to eat and enjoy some of Michelle's ghostly stories. Perhaps you'll be lucky enough to find yourself sitting next to one of the spirits of the Edmond Railyard.

OTHELLO'S ITALIAN RESTAURANT

Located just across the alleyway from the railyard is another fine eatery, Othello's. This is the second location for this business. The first was in Norman, near the OU campus. It opened its doors in 1977. After many years of success there, the owners decided to open a second location in Edmond. It opened in 2000. The owners chose for its site one of Edmond's historic buildings in the downtown area, just blocks from the UCO campus. Located at 1 South Broadway, this twelve-thousand-square-foot brick building was erected in 1910 and served as one of Edmond's first hospitals. The hospital was located on the second floor of the building; the first floor served as a movie theater. As strange as it may seem, finding a hospital on the second floor of an old building was not uncommon at that time, despite elevators being a rarity. I'm just not sure how common it was to have a movie theater located below a hospital, though. I guess that women experiencing long delivery times may have walked downstairs to see a movie to help pass

Historic Edmond Hospital, currently Othello's, Edmond. *Oklahoma Historical Society*.

the time. But what if you were at the hospital visiting a loved one taking their last breath and hearing people downstairs laughing to a comedy on the big screen? With such a diversity of emotions occurring in one space, it's no wonder this location has never found peace from paranormal activity. Unlike other locations, Othello's doesn't like to share much of its paranormal activity with the public, but the staff was kind enough to share stories and show us the old hospital location upstairs. Now housing storage rooms and offices, the hospital rooms still feature the wide doors needed to maneuver hospital beds in and out of. The space is small, consisting of only a few patient rooms and a surgical room. The hallway radiates a dark, foreboding feeling for anyone wandering there, but it's not just upstairs where the spirits roam. Strange activity has been reported throughout the building. Strange noises and dark shadows have been witnessed both upstairs and downstairs, and the apparition of a slender female has been seen looking over the upper railings, watching the customers below as they indulge themselves on delicious Italian meals. The identities of the spirits roaming the floors of this eatery are not known, but one thing is certain: They seem to enjoy being there, and it appears they have no desire to move on.

13

OKLAHOMA CITY

L ocated in the center of the state is the capital, Oklahoma City. With this city's history, it's no surprise that a good ghost story isn't too hard to find. Some of the stories are associated with locations along Historic Route 66. These are just a few of those stories.

THE SPEAKEASY OF OKC

Just north of Interstate 44, off Northwest Sixty-Third and Kelly, sits an empty building that once housed a quaint Italian eatery called Gabriella's. Locally known for its amazing food and tranquil atmosphere, it was a great place for family gatherings and nights out with friends. Gabriella's (now located in Edmond, Oklahoma) was a family-friendly place. But it wasn't always that way. For almost a century, this building has housed some of the best dining in Oklahoma City. But just prior to 1950, it was known to house a bit more. Oklahoma City has grown tremendously over the years, expanding its borders in all four directions. The building sat just northeast of the city. It was out in the country, far enough to escape the prying eyes of the law but close enough for people to join in on the lively activities. The building's notorious past began between the 1920s and 1930s. It was said to house a bordello and a speakeasy. Rumors have it that at this time, Charles Floyd, also known as "Pretty Boy Floyd," infamous gangster, was said to frequent the establishment for drinks and a game or two. In 1938, Anthony A. Manners purchased the building and renamed it the Kentucky Club. It quickly became a well-known nightclub that offered more than just an evening out. It was where a person could enjoy a night of fine dining, dancing and music. And if you knew who to ask for, you could find yourself enjoying a other nightly activities. Once you were cleared to join in on the other services the club offered, you were escorted to a secret room that housed a gambling area. You could buy a drink and enjoy the company of a lady if you so desired.

Anthony "Tony" Manners was known by local authorities as a notorious bootlegger and bookie. The Kentucky Club was often under surveillance and was raided on a regular basis. Despite the place's reputation for being a speakeasy and brothel, its clientele often consisted of not only mob bosses but also well-known political figures. It was said to have trapdoors and hidden rooms to stash booze and gambling evidence during raids. A building with such a notorious past leads one to assume that even more criminal activities took place there. For years, stories have circulated about this historic location and its haunting. It's been known by several names, including the Kentucky Club and the County Line restaurant. I'm not originally from Oklahoma, so I hadn't heard all the ghostly stories attached to this location. But I learned more when I interviewed the owner. Before I go to any haunted location, I try to avoid reading about its haunted history. This allows me to go in with an open mind and unclouded judgment. I treated Gabriella's the same way. Since the staff of most locations rumored to have a haunted history try to avoid the topic, I decided to visit and see if it was worth pursuing.

It was a chilly afternoon when my daughter Tessa and I drove to Gabriella's for dinner when the restaurant was still operating. We were the first to arrive, just as the doors were opening. The minute we stepped out of the car, we were hit with overwhelming headaches. I knew that this was going to be a great place to investigate. The building looked small and was painted white with green trim. Stepping inside, we learned that looks can be deceiving. The building stretched farther back than we anticipated. The front is a more open area that holds a few large party tables surrounded by private alcoves running along both sides of the room. There is a second room just beyond the front that opens up into another large dining area, the kitchen with an open brick oven for baking a variety of pizzas and a long wood-topped bar where patrons can sit and enjoy a cocktail. At the end of the bar is a large stone fireplace with two wingback chairs for customers to use to warm themselves by the fire.

It all appears cozy, unless of course you happen to look up and see the angry-looking man standing next to the fireplace. He was the first spirit I encountered at Gabriella's, but he was not the last. He appeared to be average height, stalky and wearing a dark suit and a fedora. He had an angry look on his face as we locked eyes. Just as quickly as he appeared, he was gone. Though I could no longer see him, I could feel his eyes boring into me. After enjoying our delicious meal, we sat down with the owner to discuss her building and the possibility of investigating it. She was more than happy to share the history of the place and some experiences since taking up residence there. I shared with the owner, Vicky, what we had already experienced in the brief time we had been there. I told her about the man standing by the fireplace. I was told that many people have reported seeing this apparition there. The story goes that a gentleman by the name of Russell was shot and killed near the fireplace, either by a fellow mobster or a jealous woman (depending on the version of the story) when he was caught flirting with a woman. As it turns out, Russell was not such a gentleman after all. Most of the paranormal activity in the building is blamed on him.

Workers have seen and heard things moving around in the bar area. Glasses are heard clinking and being thrown, as one unfortunate employee learned. She was working behind the bar area when a glass was thrown and shattered, causing a deep gash in her leg that required stitches. Russell is not the only spirit believed to haunt this historic location. Many people claim to have seen, felt and heard the disembodied voice of a woman who met her untimely demise in the basement. Legend has it that a jealous husband decapitated her after he caught her being unfaithful. To my knowledge, no evidence has been found to support these claims. But while my team was investigating this site, we did obtain what appeared to be the sound of a woman softly crying on an EVP. We also witnessed what appeared to be a shadow figure walking around the area just as our parascope equipment was responding to something. There are reports of other possible spirits in the building. I also witnessed what appeared to be a large man standing by the front door with his hands clasped in front of him. He has also been seen walking in the front area of the restaurant. A longtime employee told us that he can always tell when a paranormal investigator or psychic has visited the site. He says that the next day a strong smell of sulfur is detected. It goes away after a short time, only to come back when another investigator comes. This location has housed many businesses over the years but sits empty at this time. Many different people have come and gone, but the rich history remains. Perhaps a few of the spirits do as well.

DISTRICT HOTEL: AN OASIS WHERE YOU CAN BE YOURSELF

Standing tall in the center point of Oklahoma City's Route 66 is a hotel. It isn't just any hotel, but a special hotel shining with various colors. It's a tower of hope beckoning those who have chosen an alternative lifestyle, one that many once did not agree with. The District Hotel, once the famous Habana Inn, was purchased in 2019, before the COVID epidemic. It faced many challenges due to closures and restrictions during the pandemic. The location had been owned and operated by the same family since 1993, becoming a favorite party stop of the gay community in Oklahoma City. The building was originally erected in 1963, and the years had not been kind to it. When the new owners purchased it, it was in dire need of renovation. Unfortunately, when COVID hit, most of the owners' plans had to be put on hold because of a lack of income. Facing a complete loss of their investment, the owners came up with a plan to save the business and create a new living space for those in need of a safe and loving home. Units were soon transformed into living spaces, and tenants began to move in. The District was no longer just a hotel. Now it was a home to people facing a life on the streets after being exiled from their families, which did not accept them as they were. The District created a new family for these people, one free of judgment and full of love; a community of understanding.

Time can be an enemy to us. There is not enough time to get the job done. Time slowly ages us, wearing us down. But there is also a way that time can be good. With time comes healing. With time comes understanding. Hopefully, in time we can achieve full acceptance. But there will always be prejudice and judgment exhibited by others. It has happened time and time again in history. But with time, some things do begin to get better. The District Hotel has seen some of the worst times and has lived through them to see the light at the end of the tunnel of suppression—or in this case, the bright colors of the rainbow.

The 1980s were not kind to the gay community, and many who frequented the hotel often became victims of violence. When we think of offenders or bullies of the time, we often imagine a rural man in a "wife-beater" T-shirt. But the sad truth is that this wasn't the case. Instead, the offenders were those sworn to protect the public and uphold the law. Many lawsuits were filed against the City of Oklahoma City over the years related to discriminatory actions and physical harassment carried out by the Oklahoma City Police Department on innocent citizens who didn't quite fit the mold. Most cases were settled out of court, but considering the era, I'm not sure how much justice was served. Many innocent men and women lost their lives due to ignorance and stupidity. Some of the offending officers were known to be closeted gay men. One officer had ties to another famous Oklahoma case of misjustice and murder, but I will save that story for my next book, *Misjustice and Murder: The Karen Silkwood Case.* Perhaps the offending officers felt threatened by the thought of a gay man suddenly "making them gay," as if it was a virus of some type. Perhaps the officers were in denial of their own feelings. Whatever the causes, as a result of those actions, stricter laws have been put in place to protect members of the LGBT community.

With the COVID pandemic starting to ease up, the economy has begun to regain a foothold as people attempt to return to normal lives. The District Hotel resumed its renovation, the biggest the hotel has ever seen. New events are offered weekly, including shows, games and music. It is considered the largest gay resort in the Southwest. Most hotels have some haunted history associated with them. When one considers the number of guests who frequent hotels over many years and the deaths that occur in many hotels, whether from natural causes or foul play, these locations are bound to retain some negative energy. The District Hotel is no exception. And with its recent reconstruction, a boost of paranormal activity is to be expected. I personally have no knowledge of any deaths at this location, but further investigation may uncover some. For a hotel to be haunted, it isn't necessary that a death occurred at that exact location. There are several ways for a place to be haunted, by both the dead and the living.

Most people believe that a traumatic event or a sudden death is required to create a haunting. That is far from the truth. Even if someone did not die on the property, their spirit may return there because of memories it created or a feeling of happiness the person felt when they visited. (I personally wish to haunt Scotland after I die, since I can't afford to visit now.) So, in theory, a spirit may return to the place that meant so much to them when they were alive. But what if someone haunting a location is not even dead? Another theory, one I subscribe to, is that a person may in fact haunt a location while they are alive. Such hauntings are considered photographic hauntings. A photographic haunting is one in which the image or energy of a person is left in a place, like a stamp or a photograph replaying over and over in a loop. This often occurs when an individual experiences some kind of emotion that causes their energy to illuminate enough to create a photo-like impression on that area's time and space. As small crystal particles on a CD retain sounds and images, certain areas around the world contain enough crystal energy to create the same effect—a photographic haunting.

Some people may not be aware that they left an energy stamp at a location, but many others will witness it for years to come.

Paranormal activity has been reported in the hotel and on its grounds over the years, from disembodied voices to shadow figures. Strange noises, feelings of being watched or never being alone, objects moving and the sound of disembodied footsteps have all been reported. With such a long and colorful history, is it any wonder that spirits might wander the halls of this hotel? I know that if I had faced a life of segregation and ridicule and then found a place offering a safe and welcoming home, I'd be eager to return, even if my body was no longer around to take me there. Perhaps these spirits see this place as their own personal oasis and simply wish to make it their home. It is a safe oasis where they can forever be themselves at the District Hotel on Historic Route 66.

National Cowboy Museum

Another location rumored to be haunted along Route 66 in Oklahoma City is the National Cowboy Museum. Founded in 1955, the museum showcases various exhibits depicting the American cowboy way of life, as well as works of art, artifacts and literature, to remind us of the life of those who braved the untamed West, building a new life for themselves and surviving difficulties that lifestyle brought. Along with the exhibits, the museum offers a dining area, a ballroom and a gift shop. The museum's culture and information are shared with a guest who has wandered its halls for over half a century. Like most hotels, museums are often found to be haunted. Whether it is because of the building's history as a previous business, the land it sits on or the items it holds, a museum is always a great place to investigate hauntings and images from the past. My team has investigated many historical sites and museums over the years, and each location offers an experience all its own. The Cowboy Museum is no different. I haven't had the pleasure of investigating this site, but I have visited it for a gala or two. The building offers the curious visitor the chance to wander its halls in search of spirits. When I spoke to the curator, he chuckled a little and denied knowing any specifics of ghostly activity or encountering any himself, but he did acknowledge that others believe spirits reside there. Not having conducted a controlled investigation at the site, I can't personally guarantee that any paranormal activity has taken place. But my memories of visiting the museum have left me longing to investigate it one day. I would like to determine if what I felt was in fact a ghostly presence lingering in the halls of this amazing museum. Whether you are in search of history or the possibility of running into a ghost, the next time you find yourself driving on Route 66, stop in at the National Cowboy Museum and take a peek at what this location has to offer as it helps to keep history alive in the Wild West.

14

BETHANY

LAKE OVERHOLSER

Lake Overholser is divided between Canadian County and Oklahoma County as you travel along Historic Route 66. To the west side of the lake is the Canadian County section. Here you will find a floating dock from which people can fish, often catching small carp and catfish and, once in a while, small bass. A playground is just across the road, and ducks and geese roam around the ponds and lake. This lake is a popular area for bicyclists and motorists who want to go out for a ride on a warm sunny day. It is also a popular area for joggers, who can enjoy a more scenic run.

Built in 1918, Lake Overholser was constructed to help provide an adequate supply of water for the water treatment plant. Bethany relied heavily on the North Canadian River and local ground wells for much of its water. As population increased, so did the need for more fresh water. The idea for a manmade lake was brought up, and construction began. In 1923, the Canadian River flooded, inundating much of the city. It became evident that a new dam, bigger and more efficient, was needed. Designed by Neils Ambursen and constructed by Ambursen Construction Company of New York, the dam is 68 feet high and 1,650 feet long. It consists of buttressed spillways, a solid spillway, a concrete walkway across the dam and a brick-walled pump house. The lake was named after Edward Overholser, the sixteenth mayor of Oklahoma City and son of Henry Overholser, one of the founding fathers of Oklahoma City. Ed Overholser, born in Kansas, arrived in Oklahoma City in 1890 and took over the running of the Overholser Opera House. He helped to organize the towns of Stroud, Wellston, Luther and Jones. He became a member of the school board and later the chairman of the Board of County Commissions for Oklahoma County.

Lake Overholser is relatively small, its maximum depth reaching just thirteen feet with an average depth of about six feet. Its surface area is about 1,500 square acres, making its shore about seven miles long. Despite its size, it is a great place to visit, sit next to the water, drop a line or go for a jog. It is considered one of the most scenic areas along Route 66, which runs right through it. The days can be peaceful, and visitors can sit on the shoreline, feeling the cool breeze carried across the water while local wildlife goes about its daily routines. Ducks glide across the water, dipping their heads beneath the waves in hope of catching a meal while a few feet away the sound of a small fish jumping up out of the water can be heard. It's a nice place to visit with the kids for a fun day in the sun, but come nightfall, you may want to pack up and leave. The lake can take on a different atmosphere at night.

Lake Overholser turned one hundred years old in 2019. In the past century, the lake has seen many tragedies. And from strange lights to the ghostly image of woman walking along the shoreline, this lake has no shortage of ghostly apparitions. I was told a story by a man named Bill. (He did not want me to use his full name.) Bill told me that he used to fish late in the evening, just off the fishing dock. He often sat and watched the sun go down, enjoying the peacefulness that settled across the lake. He shared with me a frightening experience he had in April 2003. That day was like any other—at least he thought it was. He had just gotten off work after a very stressful day and thought he would swing by the lake to do a little evening fishing before heading home. He often kept his fishing things in the trunk of his car, as fishing was one of his favorite pastimes. Bill, not married at the time, wasn't in a rush to get home, so he grabbed a few snacks and headed to his favorite spot on the lake. The sun was just disappearing below the horizon. Bill kicked back in his chair with his line in the water, taking in the sounds of the water hitting softly against the rocks of the shoreline. It was early in the season, so there weren't many people around the lake. He was getting ready to pack up and head home when he noticed someone standing just down the shoreline from him. It was a pretty girl, perhaps in her mid-twenties, with long dark hair. She was staring off across the lake, as if deep in thought.

"She seemed so sad," Bill told me. "With it getting so late and dark, I was worried about her being out there all alone." So he called out to her. He said he tried calling out several times, but she didn't look over. He decided to approach her to see if there was anything he could do. Maybe she needed a lift somewhere, as he didn't notice another car or person around. He put his things into his car and headed over to her. He said he was about twenty feet away when he called out to her again. This time, she turned to look at him. He could see a thick line of blood running down the right side of her face. Their eyes met; then she disappeared. There was no sound of a splash, no sound of running footsteps. Where had she gone? "I was scared to death," Bill told me. "I knew what I had seen, but I couldn't explain what had just happened. One minute she was there, and the next she was gone." Bill says he still goes out to the lake to fish, but he has never seen the ghostly lady again. Then again, when the sun starts to set, Bill packs up and leaves. No longer does he stay past nightfall. But he says that to this day, he still wonders what or who he saw that night.

The next encounter I learned about is in the form of an otherworldly paranormal experience. It comes from a young couple who set out to enjoy some alone time on the lakeshore late one night. The young couple, in their late teens, decided to park by the lake after catching a late-night movie and grabbing a bite to eat. They weren't ready to end their date just yet, so they thought a trip to the lake would be nice on a warm summer evening. They parked on the west side of the lake. They had been there a little while and were enjoying the night sky when they noticed a bright light just above them. Thinking it was a plane flying by, they didn't pay much attention to it. There was a small airport nearby, and it was normal to see small planes overhead, especially on a clear night. They continued with their conversation, making plans to see each other the following weekend, when they looked up again and saw the same bright light. It had not changed its position. It was too large to be a star and too still to be a plane. Suddenly, the light split off into three separate lights, shooting off into three different directions. The couple stayed at the lake for another hour or so, but the strange lights never returned.

Unfamiliar lights in the sky aren't the only strange sights reported at Lake Overholser. A few years ago, a man was visiting the lake late at night. He was riding his motorcycle around the lake, taking in the spring-like weather, which was happening for the season. He was just rounding the turn by the dam when he looked out across the lake and noted a red ball hovering just above the water. He pulled over to the side of the road to get a better look at what he was seeing on the lake. No boats were on the water, and no one was fishing in that area. He could see the red reflection on the water as it slowly came toward him. He started to walk to the shoreline when he heard the screeching of tires and the sound of a truck engine close by. He turned to see the driver lose control of the truck as it took the curve too fast and swerved to the side of the road where he had been standing. The truck missed his bike by inches. Had he not been distracted by the lights and gotten off his bike to get a better look, he would have been hit by the truck as he rode his bike.

Was the mysterious light a warning or a spirit helping to detour the motorist from ending up injured or killed? Since the lake opened, many deaths have occurred there, several in recent years. From 2007 to 2013, reports ranging from accidental drownings to murder have appeared in local newspapers and on television. Are the spirits of the lake's victims still trapped here? Do they even realize that they have perished? Do they stay around to help warn others of impending death? Maybe they want to protect others from meeting the same untimely death they experienced. Do visitors from other planets frequent our skies, watching us? Whatever the truth is, a visit to Lake Overholser is a nice getaway from the hustle and bustle of city life. Just make sure to keep your eyes open. You never know what or who you might see.

BETHANY CHILDREN'S HOSPITAL AND REHAB CENTER

Located just east of Lake Overholser is Bethany Children's Hospital and Rehab Center. But the facility didn't start out as a hospital. It began as an orphanage. In 1898, a lady by the name of Mattie Mallory started opening orphanages in the Oklahoma City area. In 1909, she relocated all of the children to a centralized location, in Bethany. In 1946, the facility took on a new name, the Children's Convalescent Home. Another name change was initiated in 1951, when a new facility was built to accommodate sixty-five more beds, transforming the orphanage into the Children's Convalescent Hospital. The facility faced financial trouble in the 1970s and closure in 1975. The International Pentecostal Church assumed responsibility. With its financial help, the facility was able to stay open. In 1977, Carol and Albert Gray proved vital in turning the facility around. It stayed open for the next twenty years. In 1995, the Donald Reynolds Foundation provided a grant in the sum of just over $9.5 million to build a new complex at the campus, adding one hundred beds for inpatient care for children and teenagers. In

2008, $7 million in donations were received from the Capital Campaign, and a new Children's Center Rehab Hospital was built. In 2017, a four-story tower was erected, making the facility the largest freestanding inpatient pediatric rehab hospital in the country.

What started out as a labor of love for orphaned children progressed over the years to extend medical care to special needs children and their families. This large campus is located along the historic route just east of Lake Overholser. As a pediatric nurse who spent most of the past twenty-five years in the field, I have visited this location many times, to see a new patient or attend a therapy session with someone I was taking care of. I have also met and gotten to know several other nurses who worked there over the years. Many of them have spoken to me about the facility being haunted. One nurse told me about a hall that was no longer used due to the paranormal activity that was often witnessed there. As to the truth of that claim, I can't say, but one story I hear frequently is that of a little girl in a white dress seen roaming the halls. I'm led to believe that this spirit is of someone from the orphanage days, since many of the patients housed at the facility today are not capable of walking on their own.

Many of the young residents suffer from birth defects, many which can be fatal or can shorten a life at the least. That's the hardest part about this field of nursing. It's so difficult to lose a patient at a young age. We expect the end of life in our older patients, and I have sat at the beds of many older people as they took their final breaths, my father and my father-in-law included. Losing any patient, especially if it's a family member, is difficult. To lose a child you helped to care for is devastating. They become part of your family, and you carry them forever in your heart. So imagine a building filled with innocent little lives making the best of it from day to day, and the nurses, doctors, therapists and other staff dedicating their lives to their care. And imagine as well the heartache it brings to these workers when a precious life is lost. It's those memories that live on in the walls of this facility. Some are joyful, some are sad, but they are memories all the same. They live on in Bethany Children's Hospital and Rehab Center on Historic Route 66.

St. Joseph's Orphanage Asylum

Located about a mile up the road along Route 66 sits a venue that once served as St. Joseph's Orphanage Asylum and Industrial School. Built shortly after

Oklahoma became a state, this facility functioned as an orphanage among other things for the next sixty years. It was founded by the Roman Catholic Church of Oklahoma. John M. Kekeisen was appointed the first director when the doors opened in 1912. That year, the Sisters of Mercy arrived to receive and care for the children in the facility. In 1921, the need arose for infant and elder care. The site was renovated and renamed St. Joseph's Orphanage and Home for the Aged. It cared for more than five thousand children over the next sixty years. In 1965, the orphanage was relocated to a new site in northeast Oklahoma City. The former facility stood empty for the next three years. It was purchased by the International Pentecostal Holiness Church and used as administrative offices. It was later converted into Christian College, which is located there to this day.

Sitting just southwest of an old cathedral is the original location of Resurrection Cemetery. It is here that many of the nuns and priests who cared for the children, along with some of the children themselves, were buried. The cemetery also included a few elderly patients who resided at the facility when it became a home for the aging. Evidence has been discovered by a local writer and friend of mine, Marilyn A. Hudson, that other bodies were laid to rest in the cemetery not connected to the facility. Unfortunately, most vital records indicating the names of those buried here and how many were destroyed in a fire in the 1950s. This leads us to the next interesting turn of events. The cemetery that housed so many bodies for almost a century was purchased by the City of Bethany, which relocated the graves and built a park on the site. A monument remains, dedicated to the staff. A few names are inscribed there. A tombstone set flat into the ground in the ground is also still there today. A piece of an old iron fence remains tangled among the trees. The fence once marked the outline of someone's final resting place. Considering these factors, and

St. Joseph's Orphanage, Bethany.
Oklahoma Historical Society.

recognizing that the documents needed to prove how many people were buried here and the exact location of each grave were lost, how is it that the city was able to locate and relocate each grave? After all, the graves had occupied their spaces for more than sixty years. Like any curious paranormal investigator, I set out to see this location for myself. It was difficult to find at first, despite being in the middle of a neighborhood. But my husband and I were able to drive around enough to locate the correct street. It's an active park with a playground, basketball courts, a soccer field and a large hill of dirt and grass. And of course there are a few headstones here and there. To most people, this site wouldn't seem out of the ordinary. But for those who know its history, it's a strange feeling to watch a group of people walking their dogs, kicking a soccer ball and playing basketball on the same land that once held and perhaps still holds a cemetery.

My husband and I decided to walk around to see if we could locate the memorial marker said to be in the area. We decided to climb the tall hill to get a bird's-eye view of the layout of the land. As visitors and children playfully rolled down the hill, all I could imagine were the bodies that must still reside there, unknown to the people playing above. Wishing I had brought my investigation tools with me, I decided to use the only one accessible at the time. I turned on my ghost radio and proceeded to walk around the grounds. Immediately, words began to appear on the screen, and I soon began to ask a series of question. "Is there any bodies still buried here?" I received an immediate response: "numerous." "Could the spirit give me their names?" I received another immediate response: "Kansas." I brushed it off as a random response, and my husband made a silly *Wizard of Oz* joke about us not being in Kansas anymore. We began to drive to the other side of the park, continuing our search for the memorial. As we drove, I pored over websites, including online historical records, looking for any other information about the location. That is when I came across some historical documents, including a document listing the names of five of the nuns who had lived here and cared for the children. Listed on the website of the 1920 U.S. Census were the names of five sisters. The third name listed was that of Sister Mary Ambrose. Next to her name was one word: *Kansas*. Were the spirits of the orphanage trying to reach out to us to let us know that their bodies remained there? Or are the spirits merely continuing to inhabit the grounds of this cemetery turned city park? Perhaps we will discover the truth. Or maybe the spirits will continue to leave us clues to follow as we seek answers about the mysteries surrounding the cemetery at St. Joseph's.

15

YUKON

A s you travel farther west along Route 66, leaving the town of Bethany behind, you will find yourself entering the city of Yukon. The city is known for its annual Czech Festival in the historic district on Route 66. The event offers visitors a chance to savor specialty foods from around the world, shop local vendors and enjoy music and dance in true Czech Fest fashion. Vendors, food trucks and various acts and entertainment offer everyone a chance to enjoy something special. Historic buildings line the route, some dating back to before Oklahoma statehood. Many house businesses open to the public, offering visitors a chance to see the craftsmanship of these buildings. One such building stands on the northwest corner of the 400 block of Main Street. It's a quaint shop called Lost in Time Antiques. The owners were gracious enough to share some of the store's history and ghostly stories with us.

LOST IN TIME ANTIQUES

Built shortly after the land rush of 1889, this two-story building has survived the crushing hand of time. Wind, rain, ice, tornados and even fire could not destroy this beautifully maintained structure. Over the years, various businesses have called this building home, but today it houses Lost in Time Antiques. The building was purchased in 1996 by its current owner, and Lost in Time opened its doors a year later to patrons. Filled with antiques from all over the world, this shop offers clients a chance to admire and purchase unique and rare items. Many pieces date back almost two hundred years, and some originated in Europe. The pieces are a sight to behold, lining the old walls, which stretch back along narrow pathways deep into the building. Outside, toward the east back end of the building, a black door can be seen. Within it, a slender staircase leads to the second floor directly above the shop. On the second floor is a single apartment once used as a residence for the current owners, but they have long since moved into a home away from the store. With the building having survived for almost 124 years, the matter of it being haunted is a simple one. It is. There have been various accounts of activity over the years, from disembodied footsteps going up and down the stairs when no one was around, to running water being heard. Many have reported feeling like they are never alone, and some people feel as if someone is staring at them, boring eyes into their very souls. Perhaps the most disturbing report is that of a woman seen upstairs staring out of one of the apartment windows on the far north side. Her identity is unknown, but her presence has been witnessed by many people over the years. Perhaps she's simply residing in what used to be her home, or maybe she traveled across the ocean with one of the antique items from Europe. Whatever the case may be, it appears she has found herself a place to call home, in the upstairs apartment of Lost in Time Antiques on haunted Oklahoma Route 66.

STAGE DOOR THEATRE

Tucked away one block in from old Route 66 on Sixth Street in Yukon is a historic building. Laughter used to fill the building when it housed the Stage Door Theatre. For thirty years, cast members and crew brought laughter and tears to thousands of people, until its closure in 2016. I was blessed to be part of the last play produced in the old building, and I have had several paranormal experiences over the years, both behind the stage and throughout the building.

This historic building was erected in 1907 as one of Yukon's original schools. In the mid-1980s, the Stage Door Theatre was formed and began its lease of the building. This two-story structure consisting of several large and small rooms as well as a large basement has fallen into disrepair. The roof's several leaks have caused mold to grow throughout the building. Panels that once lined the ceilings now lay in crumbled piles as paint bubbles and peels from the walls. It was in this building that I first began my career in paranormal research.

When I first entered the building in 2008, I knew it had activity. You could feel the energy in the air. Until then, I had only read about the paranormal. I had my first paranormal experience at the age of six years old, and since then, I had been curious about the supernatural field. Although I had always had an interest in the field, I had never had the opportunity to participate in research. Little did I know that when I walked into that old brick building, my entire world would change.

I hadn't been involved with community theater since I was a teenage in California, and I decided it would be fun to do it again. I took my teenage daughter to the local community theater to audition for a role for an upcoming play. I can still remember my feelings when I stepped into the old building. There was no mistaking the fact that it was haunted. I still remember the look on our guide, Rosemary's, face as she led me and my daughter up the stairs. I asked her point-blank if the building was haunted. She simply turned to me and smiled. That was answer enough.

The current building was not the first one erected on the site. Another school was built on the property before 1907, but it burned down. We are unsure if anyone has passed away on the current property, but we do know that several spirits inhabit the building. There have been several reports of disembodied voices, full-body apparitions and knocks heard in the building. Among these spirits is a little boy that we called "Bobby."

Bobby has often been seen running around the basement area that used to be the school's gym, but he didn't stay only in that area. When I was teaching medical assistance students, some asked to go along on an investigation. I decided to take a group one night to show them how we ran our investigations. That night, Bobby was feeling friendly. A group of us were sitting down in the basement. One of my students, Tia, and I were looking down the hallway toward the large backrooms when we saw Bobby run across the hall. He was a small, slender boy dressed in early twentieth-century clothing. He reminded me of a newspaper boy. He had dark black hair and was between six and eight years old. It was the first time I had ever seen Bobby. Tia and I turned to each other in shock as we confirmed what we had just seen. Years later, I was going through old photo SD cards when I found something I had missed all those years ago. In one photo, in an upstairs room staring back at me was the small, pale face of Bobby.

Bobby was not the only spirit who resided in the building. Cast members have reported being alone in the building, working upstairs in the costume area, when they heard someone knocking at the door. When they went to answer it, no one was there. One director reported that when she was leaving the building one night, she had an eerie felling and turned around to see a woman in period costume staring back at her from the glass door. Another spirit often felt and heard was that of a little girl. I was alone in the building one day to set up for an event. I stepped into the restroom when I suddenly heard the giggle of a little girl coming from the other stall. The building was completely empty, and the doors had remained locked. Among the spirits and occurrences noted in the building, one of the most prominent is that of a dominant male figure. Many people reported feeling what seemed to be a strong presence, an authoritative spirit. It was mainly felt on stage or in the green room. At one point, I had seen a man in his mid-fifties standing on stage with his arms crossed over his chest, staring out at me sitting in the audience area. I always felt his authoritative presence, like that of a teacher or a principal—someone who demanded respect.

The strangest occurrence happened the same day I heard the little girl giggling. While I was setting up for the event, I noticed an older woman standing outside, staring up at the building. I went outside to see if I could offer any assistance. A younger woman got out of her car, and I introduced myself and asked if I could help with anything. "I brought my mom by to see her old school. I am helping her with her memoirs, and this was her old school," she told me. I asked them if they would like to come in and tour the building. They both happily replied that they would. I brought them in through the main doors and showed them around the old building, from top to bottom. After the tour, I turned to the older woman and asked, "By the way, was the school haunted when you went here?" "Not that I know of," she replied. I told her about the authoritative man I had seen and often felt in the building. I was a little surprised when the lady then told me about a principal at the school who hanged himself. Was that the man I had seen on the stage that day?

So many spirits have come and gone through the old Stage Door Theatre. Not only did it house our theater group, but it also housed the Yukon Historical Society, which filled its rooms with personal items from residents who had passed, as well as a military tombstone. The building also housed the Veterans Museum. This museum included a collection of personal military memorabilia collected over the years. Among its items were the medical bag and surgical instruments of Yukon's first doctor, as well as several pieces of equipment from his office. The theater group's stage props, clothes and costumes come from previous owners, bought from various residents from around the area. How many of these items could have had energy attached to them? We may never know the exact number of spirits that resided or may still reside at this location. But I hope that one day someone will restore this old building to its glory days and once again welcome laughter and life inside its walls.

16
EL RENO

FORT RENO

During the Indian Wars, in 1874, Fort Reno was established as a temporary military camp to protect the Cheyenne Arapaho Agency at Darlington. The camp functioned as the "Camp near the Cheyenne Agency" for five months shy of two years under Fifth Infantry and Sixth Cavalry soldiers prior to the expansion of the camp and naming of the fort. In February 1876, General Philip Sheridan named the permanent military post Fort Reno, honoring his close friend, Major General Jesse L. Reno, of Virginia, who had been killed during the Civil War. Sheridan's headquarters, a small log cabin structure, now sits on the property of the Canadian County Historical Museum in El Reno.

Soldiers of the fort, including cavalry and infantry units, Buffalo Soldiers, Cheyenne and Arapaho Indian scouts and members of the U.S. Marshals Service, were charged with policing the area of unassigned lands prior to the land runs of 1889, 1892 and 1894. The only battle near the fort was the Battle of Sand Hill in 1875. From 1892 to 1908, troops from Fort Reno were utilized in political disputes, the Spanish-American War in Cuba, rebellions among Indians and the maintenance of order during land runs. The fort ended as an active military post in 1908.

In 1908, the same year the fort ceased as an active military base, it was reactivated by the U.S. Army as a remount station. The fort was now used to train mules and horses for military duty. These service animals were used in World Wars I and II and the Korean War. Trained horses and mules were shipped to other countries for use by Allied forces, often accompanied by Fort Reno remount troops. The fort grounds were also home to polo competitions, horse races, shows, auctions and community activities. Following the end of World War II, Fort Reno was closed, in 1948, and turned over to the United States Department of Agriculture (USDA). It has since been the home of the USDA's Grazinglands Research Laboratory and hosts the Visitor's Center and Museum.

The Visitor's Center and Museum is a remodeled officer's quarters that hosts hundreds of visitors each year. This two-story building is now home to historical photos, service uniforms and weapons from the fort's functioning days. Visitors and staff have reported a feeling of being watched while in the building. If you stay long enough, you might hear the chatter of voices of people long ago or footsteps of an unseen visitor. Patrons have even reported feeling as if their hair was being pulled as they tour the site.

Located three miles west and two miles north of present-day El Reno, Fort Reno includes many original buildings that are still standing. Some have been restored and are open for tours. The Visitor's Center and Museum, the Cavalry Museum, the Chapel and the Fort Reno Cemetery are open to the public. Other structures on the property include officer's quarters, a Victorian-style home, a commissary-armory and a barn. Considering Fort Reno's history, it's no surprise that stories of unconventional visitors are told. You won't find the names of these visitors in a guest registration book, but you might see the names on a tombstone in the fort's cemetery.

WELCOME CENTER AT FORT RENO

As you exit the highway and pass through the gates to head back toward the fort, you're met with open fields stretching for miles. Cattle graze nearby, and you might be lucky enough to see a large red-tailed hawk swooping down to catch its lunch. It's a peaceful place now, much different than what it must have been like many years ago. The fort started out as a temporary camp in July 1874 to protect the Cheyenne Arapaho Agency after the Red River War of 1874. It was named after Jesse L. Reno, killed in the Civil War in South Mountain, Maryland.

The first exercise of the fort was to police the Cheyenne Arapaho Reservation. Duty called again in 1878, when the Northern Cheyenne

Welcome Center, Fort Reno, El Reno.

arrived. In late summer 1878, following a long, harsh winter, many Cheyenne perished at Darlington due to poor medical attention, inadequate food and disease. Little Wolf, tired of the mistreatment of his people, went to Agent John Miles to ask about the tribe leaving, in hopes of returning to their homeland. His plea fell on deaf ears, and his request was denied. Little Wolf was quoted as saying to Miles, "Now listen to what I say to you, I am going to leave here; I am going north to my own country." In the late hours one night, Chief Little Wolf and Chief Dull Knife led a band of Indians and fled from the reservation to head north to their homeland. The troops of Fort Reno now faced a new challenge. Captain Joseph Rendlebrock, along with two cavalry units, pursed the Native Americans in an attempt to bring them back to the reservation. The cavalry troops were up for a long battle. Under the leadership of Little Wolf, the Cheyenne were able to keep their enemy at bay despite their limited numbers. Several battles were won by the Cheyenne due to Little Wolf's superior tactical leadership. Rendlebrock became known for being the master of retreat and was later court-martialed and dismissed from service.

In the 1880s, the troops at Fort Reno, along with Indian scouts, played a major role in searching out and arresting those who illegally entered the territory prior to the land run. At that time, many "Boomers" tried to sneak into the area to stake claims to the best lands prior to the actual opening. The troops were called out again to assist with the official land run of 1889. By the end of the 1800s, Fort Reno's mandate to maintain peace on the Indian frontier had faded away. With the Spanish-American War of 1898, much of the cavalry and infantry marched away to assist in the fight. In 1908, the fort closed as an active military base. That year, the military reopened the fort as a remount station for cavalry horses and mules. Under the leadership of Majors Daniels and Weeks, along with Captain Hardeman, the fort was refurbished and expanded. Soon the fields were filled with military horses and mules that would be used in future wars. In 1948, the fort was transferred to the U.S. Department of Agriculture and remains so to this day.

Today, Fort Reno is open to tourists who wish to take a step back in time and see a bit of what life was like for the cavalry during the Indian Wars. The first building you come to after driving down the long entry road is the Visitors Center. It is here that you check in. It's a small building, whitewashed with a small covered porch. It was built in 1936 as an officer's quarters.

When you enter the building, you are greeted with a small reception area with a glass case filled with small objects for purchase, souvenirs to help you remember your trip to the fort. Lining the walls are books and goods for sale that tell of the fort's past. Off to the left is a beautiful wooden staircase leading to the second floor. As you walk toward the staircase, you come to an entryway. To the right is a door leading down to the basement. Also to the left is another open room. There you will find a large round table stacked with books and photo albums on display, open and ready to illustrate Fort Reno's past.

As you ascend the winding staircase, you enter a narrow hallway. All of the rooms have wood floors, and the creaking of the wood echoes throughout the building as you pass from one room to the next. Various artifacts are displayed around the building. There are officers' boots, uniforms and even bunks, all illustrating how officers live at the fort. Jim Johnston has volunteered off and on for the fort since 1989. As a current member of the board, Jim spends his Tuesdays in the Welcome Center. I asked Jim about the reports of paranormal activity in the building. I had heard over the years about encounters described by eyewitnesses, and I was curious to know if he had had any experiences. Jim shared a few of stories regarding the buildings around the fort. He shared one woman's experience when visiting the center. She was walking around the building, looking at the artifacts, when she suddenly felt a forceful tug on her head. She turned to see who was there but saw no one. She quickly ran downstairs to report what had happened. Other reports over the years have involved hearing footsteps upstairs as if made by a heavy boot. Cold spots have been reported throughout the building, and people report the feeling of being watched. Many believe that the building is haunted by a lieutenant colonel who supposedly committed suicide in the upstairs bathroom by shooting himself in the head. One story even went on to state that repairs were made to patch the bullet hole in the ceiling.

Do soldiers still walk the narrow halls of the Welcome Center or pull the hair of unsuspecting visitors? Perhaps you will have a paranormal experience when you visit Fort Reno. It is definitely a trip worth taking.

CAVALRY MUSEUM AT FORT RENO

The Cavalry Museum, open to visitors, is the oldest structure on the Fort Reno grounds. It was built as a duplex to house officers and their families. The structure was used in this capacity from 1876 to 1948. It then sat vacant for many years. Finally, in 2014, as the building neared demolition, the U.S. Cavalry Association raised funds to restore the building. It opened to the public in April 2015. The Cavalry Museum at Fort Reno is now the national headquarters for the U.S. Cavalry Association and houses items from saddles to uniforms and many other service-related artifacts. The museum stands just east of the parade grounds and south of the Visitor's Center and Museum. The restored two-story building features an enclosed porch that spans the entire front of the house. When you enter the building, you see that the structure was restored with great care, from the original wood finishes to the artifacts displayed. In the front, you are greeted by a set of stairs that lead to the second floor. Just to your right is an open archway leading into a large open room filled with artifacts and memorabilia available for purchase. You will also find your tour guide there, ready to assist you and answer any questions. When you start the tour, you are led upstairs and shown though various rooms. This building was once a duplex housing unit, and signs of that can be seen throughout the building. Each room has its own theme or motif, housing cases with items from the cavalry's past. From officers' living quarters to memorabilia from the Civil War, it truly is a step back in time.

Several people reported odd occurrences during the building's vacancy. A worker at Fort Reno reported seeing lights on in the building, even though there was no electricity. When restoration began on the buildings, people working on the outside of second-story windows reported seeing a lady walk through the hallway in front of them and vanish through a wall.

On many occasions, between visitation and after hours, Wendy, one of the staff members at the time, reported feeling the presence of a young child. Pencils were knocked off desks, items were moved frequently at about waist height and a flask flew off of a shelf one night when Wendy's kids were working in the office area. A volunteer leading a tour for a small family felt he might be going crazy when he heard children laughing during the tour, until the parents in the group asked him, "Do you hear kids laughing?" Burial records show that a young boy, Louis Trass, an officer's son, died in April 1900 of unknown causes. Maria Wheeler, the daughter of a widow, passed away in a fire in the home that stood just north of the museum. Her brother survived. Louis and Maria are buried next to each other in the fort's cemetery.

On one occasion, a patron of the museum was so shaken by her experience during her visit that she drove to a diner in town to write down her experience. She brought it back to the museum. Wendy said everything was normal that day. The visitors had come in and were walking through the upstairs area at a normal pace when all of a sudden they ran downstairs. The woman said she heard someone choking behind her. She turned and asked, "Are you ok?" She then realized that no one was behind her.

Before visiting the museum, I had little information about it other than that it is a cavalry museum and that the spirits of two children are likely hanging around it. When I arrived, I was invited to look around and get a feel for the building. While walking upstairs, I felt I did encounter a lady, an overseer of things. Walking through the rooms a couple of times, I heard footsteps in the room next to me, even though I was alone upstairs. I did not pick up on a young boy until a little later, as I was sitting in the office speaking with Wendy. My three-year-old was pacing back and forth, oblivious to everything. He peeked out from the hallway across from us, as if he was curious. Are the spirits of this house trying to get our attention? Are they trying to send a message? Or are they just returning to a familiar spot? Perhaps a visit to the museum will help you answer those questions.

CHAPEL AT FORT RENO

Located just northwest of the Welcome Center is an old European-style chapel. It was built in 1944 by a group of German prisoners of war. A shield of arms still graces the chapel today to remind everyone of the craftsmen who labored to build the chapel.

On July 4, 1943, during World War II, the first German POWs arrived at Fort Reno by rail. Most of the prisoners were from General Erwin Rommel's Afrika Korps, captured in North Africa. Prisoners were given jobs around the fort. Some were even hired out as farmhands to neighboring farms. The farmers paid the government $1.50 a day for prisoner labor, and in turn the government paid the prisoners $0.10 an hour in scrip money, which they could use to purchase goods at the canteen. Prisoners were allowed more freedom and luxury at the fort than American prisoners experienced in Germany. Prisoners at the fort were able to purchase two beers a day, along with cigarettes and other items. When prisoners left the fort to work on the farms, they packed a sack lunch. Many farmers provided food or snacks for the prisoners. After the war, many of the prisoners stayed in touch with their American employers. About seventy German POWs are buried at the cemetery, but only one of them died at Fort Reno. The prisoners left a lasting mark on Fort Reno, from the trees lining the entry drive to the beauty of the white chapel. Fort Reno shares a past of unity among the U.S. soldiers, the farmers and the POWs during a difficult time in our country's history.

When you arrive at the chapel, you are witness to the contrast of the chapel's white walls against a light-blue sky. The dark wooden doors with their cast-iron hinges and the square turret on the east side of the building give the chapel a medieval feel. As you ascend the set of stairs and approach the heavy wooden doors and then step through the entryway, you begin a trip back in time. Wood floors are found throughout the upstairs sanctuary. Solid, carved wooden benches line each side of the aisle. Cross timbers support the high arched ceiling, and wooden carved chandeliers adorn the hall. A wooden pulpit sits below the curved archway outlining the stage, and a wooden hand-carved cross adorns the wall directly behind it. Arched glass windows line the walls, allowing the sun to cast eerie shadows on the floor. To the front of the sanctuary and to the west of the pulpit is an open doorway. This leads to an office just behind the stage and to a narrow staircase leading into the basement area. Short ceilings and steel round beams support the sanctuary above. In the basement is a small kitchen as well as an open area to set up tables for weddings or other events. Several years ago, I chose to hold an event here.

Fascinated with some of the history as well as the paranormal stories associated with the site, I decided to hold one of our paranormal conferences at the old chapel. After the guests had left and the vendors had packed up and gone, I found myself alone in the basement of the building doing some last-minute cleaning when I heard what sounded like someone walking around upstairs. Being responsible for the site, I quickly went upstairs to see who was still in the building. The front doors remained locked, and the only way to exit was to take the stairs into the basement,

Old Mission, Fort Reno, El Reno.

the same ones I had just climbed. No one had passed me on the stairs. With the stairs being so narrow, it would be hard for someone to do it at all. I made a quick walkthrough upstairs, looking down all the aisles in the seating area, the changing room and the office. No one was in the building with me—at least, no one living. I definitely feel that I was not alone. I descended the stairs back into the basement, then climbed the outside staircase to meet the rest of my group at the car. I told them about what I had just experienced. My car was parked next to the basement door. No one had been seen entering or leaving the building. I know that I heard the heavy footsteps of an unseen presence echoing throughout the building. I have no explanation where they came from, but I do know that something or someone was there with me. Could it be the spirit of one of the prisoners who helped build the chapel so many years ago? Does the wood and mortar hold the energy of a past worker who skillfully carved the details and designs into the wood? The old chapel holds a special feeling that waits for you to pass through the archway of its wooden doors.

Fort Reno Cemetery

A short drive along a gravel road just west of the fort leads to a waist-high wall of stone surrounding Fort Reno Cemetery. The cemetery is the final resting place for military personnel and their families, civilian employees and their families and prisoners of war from World War II. Of the nearly two hundred graves, only about one-third contain soldiers, most of whom did not die in battle.

Tradition says that all cemeteries are creepy, eerie places. I find that most cemeteries are peaceful and places of rest. I had visited Fort Reno Cemetery before, during high school, and I remember it being my favorite part of the fort. I've always been a fan of old grave markers. As I walked up to the modest gate with a small sign reading "Fort Reno Cemetery," I didn't have the usual peaceful feeling. The difference may have been that I knew some of the history of the fort and its function, and let's face it, history is more appreciated with age. It was a windy day, not surprising for the Plains. I almost did not want to open the guest book and sign it for fear of pages being ripped away. But I'm glad I did sign it. Visitors from all over the country and the world have come here to pay their respects. Coins rest on gravestones, placed by men and women who have also served in the military.

I wondered about the identity of the lady in white. This spirit has been seen among the cedar trees. Is the woman buried here? During her life, did she visit a loved one buried here? Did she work at the fort? Could she be the wife of the notable Indian scout Benjamin Clark, who is interred in the fort's cemetery?

Benjamin Clark started his military career at the age of thirteen as a post courier at Fort Bridger, Wyoming. He served in the Sixth Kansas Cavalry during the Civil War, patrolling the Arkansas and Missouri borders. Following the war, Clark managed packtrains and married his first wife, a Cheyenne woman known as Emily, and had his first child, a girl, named Jennie. Emily died in January 1873. Clark remarried, to a Cheyenne woman named Red Fern with whom he had another child, Emily. Ben's second wife died in 1880, and he remarried later that year, to a woman named Moka, also known as "Little Woman." Ben Clark and Moka had twelve children, five of whom died before 1900. Clark became fluent in the Cheyenne and Arapaho languages and was respected by Indians and whites alike. He joined the U.S. Army as a scout in 1868. He served as chief of scouts for General Philip Sheridan and Lieutenant Colonel George Custer. Clark's wife died on May 6, 1913. After many years of service, the loss of his third wife and suffering from paralysis, Benjamin Clark ended his life in his quarters at Fort Reno. That building still stands today, but it is not open to the public. Staff call the building the Ben Clark House. Clark and Emily are buried in the fort's cemetery. Several people have reported a feeling of being choked when around the house.

Near the cemetery, a member of a paranormal team leading ghost tours of the fort recorded an EVP of someone saying, "I know, I know, I was run over." Searching through records, it was found that Tim O'Connell, an employee of the quartermaster department, was helping three soldiers move to the fort on January 1, 1899. One of the soldiers hopped on the back of the mule that O'Connell was riding on, startling the animal. Both riders were thrown off. O'Connell landed in front of the wagon and was killed when the wagon ran over him. He is buried in the fort's cemetery. His tombstone reads simply "O'Connell."

Perhaps the most somber aspect of the cemetery, aside from the many graves of children, is the western section. This part of the cemetery is the final resting place of 70 prisoners of war. During World War II, 1,300 POWs were brought to Fort Reno, many of them from the Afrika Korps and captured in North Africa. Many of the prisoners were hired as laborers at the fort and on local farms. Prisoners built the chapel in 1944. Of the 70 POWs buried here, only 1 died at the fort. Most of the others died in military camps around Oklahoma and Texas and were brought to Fort Reno Cemetery for burial.

Sightings of a full-body male apparition have been reported in the old Commissary and Armory building, which is not currently open to the public. Patrons and staff have reported seeing the same thing at different times of the day. Several people have seen a young man asking, "Is this a joke?" On April 24, 1885, William Stockwell, who was not feeling well, sought out the drug quinine. The only other personnel in the vicinity directed him to a bottle sitting on a windowsill. William questioned the substance but took a large dose after being assured by several comrades that the contents of the bottle was quinine. Stockwell lived just two hours after taking this fatal dose. It was later confirmed by the doctor that the bottle contained strychnine. William was twenty-five years old when he died. He is buried at the fort.

The number of children buried here, fifty-six, speaks of the mortality rate for infants and children during the time the fort was functioning. Perhaps the lady in white, seen between the trees, still watches over them.

The Haunted Highways of El Reno Route 66

Thousands of highways and roads stretch across the United States, many of them bearing witness to fatalities and injuries over the years. Crosses, flowers and memorials can be seen on the sides of roads, paying homage to family members and friends who spent their last few moments of life at or near that spot. They commemorate a life taken too soon. Despite the major changes made to Route 66, many of the victims who perished along the route continue to travel the familiar roadway, never to reach their destination but to be forever a memory of the Historic Route 66. These are a few of their stories.

Dead Man's Curve

It seems that every town has a legend of a crybaby bridge or a dead man's curve. El Reno is no different. It is interesting that an internet search for haunted locations in El Reno does not bring up many stories. But there are several haunted locations here, enough that I plan on writing my next book on the city of El Reno. You won't find many stories online about the Centre Theater or the Canadian County Museum. A story I did come across several times was about dead man's curve. The road is located just behind the old sewage plant. The plant, built in 1941, now sits abandoned. The buildings have been overrun by Mother Nature. A heap of metal stands in decay, buildings have broken windows and bricks and mortar lay on the ground. This location possesses not only an eerie beauty but also a potential danger to anyone who trespasses on this site.

The small two-lane road is located on the outskirts of El Reno. There are several versions of what occurred at this location. One version says that a van with nineteen people in it crashed when the driver tried to take the curve too fast. He lost control of the van, causing a wreck that killed all of the passengers. In another version of the story, the van had nine passengers when it wrecked. Such is the nature of most urban legends.

It is said that if you park along that road on a quiet night, you can hear the screeching of tires and the grinding of metal as if a vehicle is being torn apart. Some say you can hear the screams of the victims as they lay dying on the road. Is the memory of the incident etched into the road? Perhaps the replay serves as a caution to those who drive on the dangerous curve.

Whether the story is legend or truth, the fact remains that this section of the road is dangerous and has seen many accidents over the years. Use caution if you attempt to seek out the truth behind the legend and try to hear the bloodcurdling screams of the victims. Your speed may not be the only thing you need to be careful of on dead man's curve.

Ghostly Route 66

One story takes place on the stretch of old Route 66 between Yukon and El Reno. Several drivers have witnessed the same ghostly apparition of a man in the middle of the road. One summer night, while driving down the highway, a witness claimed to see a mist develop in the middle of the road. It was around July, and the air was dry due to a drought. The closer the witness got to the mist, the more it started to assume the outline of a man. But the mist disappeared as she drove through it. The witness later told the story to a friend, who said it reminded her of a tale of an old Native American man who was hit by a car after passing out drunk in the middle of the road. This witness wasn't the only one to see the ghostly shape. Similar stories have been told by others. One person said that they got out of their car to look for a body because they thought they had hit someone. So, if you're driving on a hot summer night along Route 66, keep an eye out for the ghost and be careful where you drive.

The Hunchback of Route 66

There is a second legend associated with a road in El Reno.

A long stretch of the highway between El Reno and Weatherford is the site of the legend of a hunchedback man. Many people have claimed to see the man. Some even claim to have given him a ride, but no one seems to know where he came from or why he chose to walk this lonely highway. He is seen wandering the road on rainy and cloudy nights. He wears a long brown trench coat with a Bogie-style hat pulled over his eyes to shield the rain from his face—or so the story goes. One unlucky driver literally ran into him one night. The woman and her son were driving on the highway when she saw the man directly in front of her car. She tried to swerve, but it was too late. She and her son felt the impact of the car hitting him. She pulled over to check on the victim, only to find no trace of him and no damage to the car.

Another person reported driving on the road when he came upon a man walking on the roadside in the rain with a brown coat pulled tightly around him. He stopped and offered the man a ride. He said that he drove with the man for a while, sharing his love of God and witnessing to him. Suddenly, the man was gone without a trace. Another driver claims that he picked up the wandering stranger on a rainy night. He says his passenger was an eerie old man who said not a word. The peculiar passenger suddenly grabbed for the door handle to jump out. The driver quickly pulled over, but the man had disappeared from his seat. The driver then passed him again a few miles down the road.

Did the man in the trench coat pass away after being hit by a car many years ago? Does he continue to relive that tragic night? Should you find yourself driving on this stretch of Route 66 on a cold, rainy night, you might want to keep your eyes open. You never know who you will run in to on the road. Perhaps you will see the famous hunchback of Route 66.

Haunted Historic Buildings on El Reno's Route 66

There are several haunted locations on El Reno's haunted Route 66, and considering the history of the town and its sordid past, it's no wonder. With so many towns along the route, I can't possibly mention them all, but a few deserve that their stories be told.

There is a building on the northeast corner of Bickford and 66. The building has been around for almost 120 years and has housed many businesses in that time. It started out as a grocery store and later housed the city library upstairs, until the Carnegie library was built a few blocks away. A more recent occupant was the old Murry Hospice office. The building is currently owned by a local attorney and his wife. It houses his law firm office and her counseling practice. Many renovations have been done in the past few years, and some work is still being done. Current renovations are being done on the third floor and at the top of the old brick building. It's on the third floor that several mysterious encounters have taken place in the past few years. There have been reports of a male spirit who tends not to like women very much, especially those who are strong-willed and independent, such as myself. You can only imagine how much he must enjoy it each time I visit. Many guests that we have taken in to participate in paranormal investigations have made note of his ominous presence, often reporting a sudden feeling of uneasiness or having a headache. The spirit has even been known to appear as a full-body apparition in a doorway at the top of the stairs. The third floor has a look and feel all its

Perkins Law Firm, El Reno.

own. Its dark hallway spans the length of the building, and small, darkened rooms are on both sides. Dust coats the walls and windowsills, each layer of dust containing a different layer of history.

Another well-known spirit is of a young woman. She has made her presence known several times. She is believed to be the spirit of a woman who worked as a lady of the night when the building was rumored to house a bordello. The third floor is not alone in playing host to spirits. The second floor has had several hauntings, including the appearance of a child who likes to interact with the equipment we bring with us. The child has even tossed things around. The spirit of a man has been seen walking up and down the back staircase, his identity unknown. Perhaps the severed hand belongs to him. When renovations were being done years ago, a crew went into the basement to fill it in with dirt. There, a severed hand was found. The sheriff's department was notified, and the hand was taken away. No further information was provided to the owners of the building at the time, and no other information has been discovered.

Among the other experiences reported in the building are loud bangs, shadow figures, disembodied footsteps, feelings of uneasiness and cold spots. The current owners have talked about renovating the upstairs and turning it into a bed-and-breakfast. I for one can't wait to stay the night if this plan ever comes to pass. The history of this building can be felt by all. The beautiful woodwork appears on each floor, the exceptional work of true craftsmen. On the south exterior wall is a mural depicting historic times along the route.

Another eye-catching attraction is a block away: a giant Route 66 sign, which glows brightly at night, making it the perfect location for a photo op with family and friends. Located just in front of that sits a small metal gate decorated with padlocks, representing different visitors' testaments to their shared love. Such sites make El Reno one of the top places to stop along Oklahoma's haunted Route 66.

17

CLINTON

Located about sixty miles west of El Reno is another town worth visiting. Clinton, founded in 1903, features the popular Route 66 Museum. The museum is part of the Oklahoma Historical Society and illustrates what it was like to travel along the Mother Road in its earlier days. The museum features a 1950s diner and exhibits regarding the Dust Bowl era. Across the street from the museum is an old motel that once served travelers along the route and even hosted Elvis Presley. The town has a selection of shops in the historic downtown area, including antiques shops. I have visited one of the antiques shops on many occasions. It is known to have ghostly inhabitants that continue to roam its storefront.

The Mulberry Bush Vintage Market at 604 Frisco Avenue is one of the town's historic brick buildings in the downtown district. With its wide wooden steps and tall ceilings, this two-story building offers vintage and antique items. They fill the space to maximum capacity. Collectibles from several eras are for sale. The market makes it easy to find the perfect item for almost anyone. The building is welcoming, and despite the spirits who seem to reside here, the space is more inviting than foreboding. From disembodied footsteps to full-body apparitions, the market offers a unique experience for those wishing to take a step back in history. I have always felt a supernatural presence when visiting this establishment. It was during my second visit that I was able to confirm my suspicion. I was upstairs, near the back of the store, looking through a box of old black-and-white photographs. I felt as if someone had walked into the small space with me. I turned to say "hello," only to find no one there. I took a step outside the room and caught a glimpse of what appeared to be a lady wearing a long, dark dress. Her hair was pinned high on her head with a few strands cascading down to her shoulders. I started walking toward her when she turned to look back at me. Just as I started to say something, she disappeared. It startled me, causing me to stare off in the direction where the apparition had been. With my eyes and mouth wide open, I knew I had just met one of the residents of the Mulberry Bush Vintage Market. Maybe one day I will see her again and be able to determine her identity and discover her story.

18

ELK CITY

One of the last moderate-sized cities along the route, just before it exits the state, is Elk City. Settlers began to inhabit the area in 1892 after the opening of the Cherokee outlet in Indian Territory. The original Great Western Cattle Trail, which extended from Texas to Dodge City, Kansas, once ran through the middle of present-day Elk City. The tent city established here was called Crowe. The townspeople later voted on a new name, choosing Busch, in the hopes that Anheuser-Busch would open one of its businesses in town. When that attempt failed, a new name was chosen. Elk City was chosen, and the name has lasted to this day.

Those days are long gone, but the history lives on at the town's museum, the Elk City Museum Complex and National Route 66 Museum. The complex features several buildings, both historic and those made to resemble buildings of the city's past. The site offers visitors a chance to experience the farm and ranch life of the settlers who arrived in western Oklahoma. Visitors can walk through the small town, looking in storefront windows and getting an idea of how life was like many years ago. You can view sculptures and other pieces of art in the art museum exhibit and take a ride in a 1955 pink Cadillac on Route 66. This museum offers fun and education for all age groups. If you're looking for the ghostly spirits of Elk City, you are sure to find some here. Spirits are especially prevalent in the main office of the museum. It is in one of the original structures purchased by the city and moved to their current location.

Old Town Museum, Elk City.

Originally the home of the Young family, this wood, two-story mansion was built in 1911 and features a wraparound porch and rooms of various sizes. O.H. Young was a wealthy businessman. He and his partner, a Mr. Herring, owned a chain of shops known as the Herring and Young Mercantile. The men had several locations in the western Oklahoma

Route 66 Auto Museum, Elk City.

region. The family occupied the home until the 1940s, when the mansion was sold to a local business, the Martin Funeral Home. The funeral home remained in the building until the mid-1960s. The city then purchased the building and relocated it to the museum site, where it sits to this day. The museum opened its doors in 1967, welcoming visitors from around the world. Charles Wren, the curator, was gracious enough to share a little of the mansion's history with me. He denies having experienced any paranormal activity. This leaves me to wonder if any paranormal activity resides within the aging timbers of the Young home. I believe that they do.

There are two locations in the home that I was particularly drawn to. The first was a room located near the entryway, just past the front desk area. As you walk through the doorway, you notice a front room area with various exhibits, including an old organ and old couches occupied by mannequins in period clothing. Perhaps the mannequins gave this area an eerie feeling. I did have the sensation of being watched as the hairs on the back of my neck stood on end. Another place of interest for me is one of the back rooms, which you come to just before you reach the stairs that lead to the second floor. Various items are displayed in wood and glass showcases in the room. Of all the rooms in the mansion, this one gave me the darkest impression. Perhaps an item stored in one of the cases contains a type of energy. Or perhaps this room was used for the preparation of bodies during the funeral home's tenure in the building. Whatever the reason, the energy is still lingering in the bones of the mansion, perhaps waiting patiently for the day it will be awakened to relive its life again.

19

OTHER NOTABLE STOPS ALONG THE WAY

There are several other stops along Route 66 that deserve a visit. These sites may or may not have a haunted history attached to them. Please look into the sites in this list to learn more about these amazing locations in Oklahoma.

The Blue Whale, Catoosa
Pops, Arcadia
The Feathery Crow, Arcadia
The Round Barn, Arcadia
Route 66 Locks of Love and Sign, El Reno
The Air and Space Museum, Weatherford
The Prairie Grill, Elk City
The Totem Pole Park, Chelsea
Golden Driller, Tulsa
Lucille's Service Station, Hydro
Native American Muffler Man, Calumet
J.M. Davis Arms and Historical Museum, Claremore
Will Roger Memorial Museum, Claremore
Chandler Route 66 Interpretive Center, Chandler
Harley & Annabelle's, Erick
Sapulpa Fire Department Museum, Sapulpa
Big Gas Pump-Kellyville
Ribbon Road-Miami/Afton
The Butcher BBQ Stand, Wellston

Blue Whale, Catoosa.

Pops, Arcadia.

This page, top: The Feathery Crow, Arcadia; *This page, bottom*: The Round Barn, Arcadia; *Following page, top*: The Fireman's Museum, Sapulpa; *Following page, bottom left*: Tallest gas pump in the world, Kellyville; *Following page, bottom right*: Ribbon Road Monument just outside Miami.

CONCLUSION

Whether you travel Historic Route 66 in search of history, folklore or phantoms, I encourage you to plan your trip and experience all the wonders you can along the way. With the ever-growing population and changing roadways, the route may soon disappear. But as long as we strive to hold on to its history, maybe we can save more of it for the benefit of future generations. So grab your friends or family, hop in your car and take to the road. You, too, can make lifetime memories on the Mother Road and get your own kicks on Route 66.

BIBLIOGRAPHY

ARTICLES

Asylum Projects. "Eastern Oklahoma Tuberculosis Sanatorium." www.asylumprojects.org.

Biography. "Bonnie Parker." www.biography.com.

———. "Charles 'Pretty Boy' Floyd." www.biography.com.

Caldwell, Bill. "Bill Caldwell: Billy Cook Lived by the Gun and Roamed." Joplin (MO) Globe, July 16, 2021.

Cosgrove, Jaclyn. "Epidemic Ignored: When Oklahoma Closed Its Psychiatric Hospitals, It Turned Patients into Inmates." Oklahoman (Oklahoma City, OK), November 13, 2016.

Cowan, Emily. "Eastern State Hospital." Abandoned OK. www.abandonedok.com.

DeFrange, Mark. "Pretty Boy Floyd's Life, Crimes Retold." Oklahoman (Oklahoma City, OK), April 26, 1992.

Discover Oklahoma. "Rock Café: Stroud." www.discoveroklahomatv.com.

Encyclopedia of Oklahoma History and Culture. "Chandler." www.okhistory.org.

———. "Claremore." Oklahoma Historical Society. www.okhistory.org.

———. "Vinita." Oklahoma Historical Society. www.okhistory.org.

Gayly. "Habana Inn Purchased: Becomes Hotel Haban." January 18, 2019.

Going, Marti. "Paranormal Exploration Set Up for Claremore Belvidere Mansion." Fox 23 News, October 7, 2022. www.fox23.com.

Haunted Places. "Rogers State University."www.hauntedplaces.org.

Haunted Rooms America. "Most Haunted Hotels in Oklahoma." www. hauntedrooms.com.

History. "FBI Agents Kill Fugitive 'Pretty Boy' Floyd." www.history.com.

———. "Tulsa Race Massacre." May 31, 2023. www.history.com.

Hudson, Marilyn A. "The 1912 to 1920 Track to the Orphanage from Current Route 66." St. Joseph Children's Home 1912–1965. www. stjosephhome.blogspot.com.

———. "Saint Joseph Orphanage: A History (Bethany, OK)." St. Joseph Children's Home: 1912–1965. stjosephhome.blogspot.com.

Justia. "State v. Powell." www.law.justia.com.

———. "United States of America, Plaintiff-Appellee, v. Jesse Eugene Tecumseh, Defendant-Appellant, 630 F.2d 749 (10th Cir. 1980)." www.law. justia.com.

KFOR. "Exclusive: Inside the Oklahoma Hospital for the Insane." May 20, 2015. www.kfor.com.

Mattingly-Arthur, Megan. "Haunted Houses by Claremore, Oklahoma." USA Today. www.traveltips.usatoday.com.

McNutt, Michael. "Mom-Killer Again Flees Mental Hospital at Vinita." Oklahoman (Oklahoma City, OK), July 6, 1991.

Never Quite Lost. "The British Airmen of Miami." July 30, 2017. www. neverquitelost.com.

News on 6. "Unmarked Graves at Eastern State Hospital Should Not Be Marked, AG Says." September 6, 2000. www.newson6.com.

Oklahoman (Oklahoma City, OK). "Vinita Still Remembers Will Rogers with Rodeo." August 13, 1989.

Only in Your State. "The Disney Movie Cars Was Inspired by Rock Café, a Small Town Oklahoma Eatery." December 18, 2019. www. onlyinyourstate.com.

Overall, Michael. "The Mosser Massacre and Tulsa's Forgotten Role in the Case." Tulsa (OK) World, January 7, 2018.

Websites

American Towns. "Bristow, Oklahoma." www.americantowns.com.

Bethany Children's Health Center. www.bethanychildrens.org.

Clinton, Oklahoma. www.clintonok.gov.

G.A.R. Cemetery. "Mrs. Frantie 'Frances' Mae Hill." www. garcemeterymiamiok.com.

Legends of America."Ghostly Tales of Oklahoma 66." www. legendsofamerica.com.

———. "Kerryville, Oklahoma: Small Town America." www. legendsofamerica.com.

Lincoln County Museum of Pioneer History. www.okpioneermuseum.com.

National Cowboy & Western Heritage Museum. www. nationalcowboymuseum.org.

Officer Down Memorial Page. "Chief of Police George Luckett." www. odmp.org.

Oklahoma Historical Society. www.okhistory.org.

Rock Café on Route 66. www.rockcafert66.com.

The Route 66. "Kellyville." www.theroute-66.com.

Route 66 Podcast. "44. Miami, OK: Royal Air Force Cadets Final Resting Place along Route 66." www.route66podcast.com.

T&M Reviews. "The Rock Café Restaurant Review." YouTube, April, 21, 2022. www.youtube.com.

Veronica. "15 Ghost Towns on Route 66." Touristear Travel Blog. www. touristear.com.

Wikipedia. "Creek County, Oklahoma." https://en.wikipedia.org.

———. "U.S. Route 66 in Kansas." https://en.wikipedia.org.

ABOUT THE AUTHOR

Tanya has been interested in the paranormal since she saw her first full-body apparition in her own home at the age of six. She started doing research on the paranormal around 2001 and joined a paranormal investigation team around 2008. She started her own paranormal investigation team, the Oklahoma Paranormal Association (OPA), in 2011. As the founder of OPA and president of Paranormal Times Entertainments LLC, she is always teaching others and providing investigations for public and private institutions. She has been featured on Syfy and Travel Channel shows *My Ghost Story, Paranormal 911* and *Haunted Hospitals,* as well as in many articles, podcasts and newscasts. She has co-authored many books, including *Haunted Guthrie, Haunted Canadian County, Haunted Shawnee Oklahoma* and *Haunted Oklahoma City.* Along with speaking at a number of paranormal events in Oklahoma, she has started teaching her first paranormal class, Paranormal Psychology, at Francis Tuttle Metro Technology Center. She hopes to develop a special textbook for future classes. She has a bachelor's degree in parapsychology and is currently working toward her PhD. Aside from investigating the paranormal, Tanya has been a pediatric nurse for the past twenty-one years and works with special needs children. She is a published children's book author. Her latest publication is an adapted version of *Haunted Oklahoma City,* Spooky America's *Haunted Oklahoma City.* She is continuing to add to her book series, which will focus on her two favorite topics, history and the paranormal. She is also writing a fiction mystery novel, several children's books, a metaphysical collection and a true-crime book of historic significance.

FREE eBOOK OFFER

Scan the QR code below, enter your e-mail address and get our original Haunted America compilation eBook delivered straight to your inbox for free.

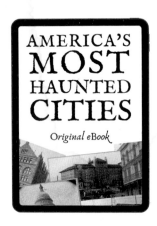

ABOUT THE BOOK

Every city, town, parish, community and school has their own paranormal history. Whether they are spirits caught in the Bardo, ancestors checking on their descendants, restless souls sending a message or simply spectral troublemakers, ghosts have been part of the human tradition from the beginning of time.

In this book, we feature a collection of stories from five of America's most haunted cities: Baltimore, Chicago, Galveston, New Orleans and Washington, D.C.

SCAN TO GET
AMERICA'S MOST HAUNTED CITIES

Having trouble scanning? Go to:
biz.arcadiapublishing.com/americas-most-haunted-cities